The Oracle of Malachi

The danger of being disappointed with God

By Pastor Jerry Marshall

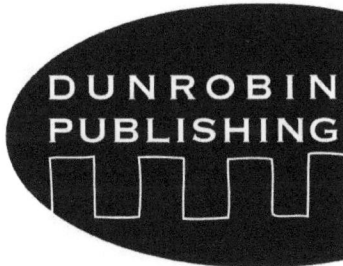

DUNROBIN PUBLISHING

Permission to quote in critical reviews with citation:
The Oracle of Malachi
By Pastor Jerry Marshall

ISBN 978-0-9832363-3-7 paperback

Printed in the United States by Dunrobin Publishing

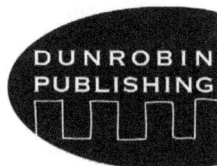

DUNROBIN
PUBLISHING

Dunrobin Publishing
www.dunrobin.us

CONTENTS

__Introduction__

After reflecting upon all that God has done for us and given to us as an expression of His super abundant grace, you would think it would be easy to give our all to His purposes and will. Yet many of us who profess to possess a life-transforming relationship with the living Lord seem fine with giving Him far less than our best. How is it that we can become comfortable with the notion that partial obedience is obedience to the Lord? Or, that halfhearted devotion is a sufficient level of dedication to the One who has demonstrated that He was willing to lay down His life in pursuit of our best.

It has been my burden throughout my pastorate to probe this strange form of "devotion" to God and what needs to be done to be able to sing with integrity, "All To Jesus I Surrender." I know from personal experience that there are many barriers to remaining steadfast in your devotion to the Lord. We learn from the Word of God that this "present age," with its floating mass of ever evolving worldviews, ethics and values, can easily capture our hearts if we are not on guard. This is what robbed the devotion of a man called Demas from serving the Lord with all his heart even though he was a fellow missionary and companion of the apostle Paul (2 Timothy 4:10).

The Bible warns us not to love this world or the things of this world (1 John 2:15-17). Paul exhorted the Romans not to allow this present age to conform them into its mold (Romans 12:2). James said that if we become a friend of this world, we become an enemy of God (James 4:4). When Jesus prayed for His disciples, He stated that those who belong to Him are in this world and yet, not of it (John 17:14-16). When we accommodate the values of this present age, we can be sure that our dedication to Christ and His purposes will be far less then what He deserves.

Another barrier to maintaining singular dedication to Christ occurs when relationships with people become greater in importance than our relationship with the Lord. This is why Jesus demanded of His disciples that He would be the possessor of their supreme affection. Because if you love people more than you love the Lord, you will compromise your relationship with our Savior and submit to the necessary requirements for maintaining those valued horizontal relationships (cf. Luke 14:25-26; Matthew 10:23-39; John 12:42-43).

When we forget the nature of our relationship with Him, compromise is inevitable. He is Lord and Master and we are His slaves. We are to be about doing His will. We are not to assume that He must assist us in accomplishing our desires and purposes. We are to serve Him. The Lord is not some sort of cosmic genie who must meet our desires in order to secure complete dedication from us.

He gave His life for us so that we might live for Him (2 Corinthians 5:14-15; 1 Corinthians 6:19-20). Love, and the abundance of mercy that we have received, should compel us to present ourselves to Him as a living sacrifice (Romans 12:1).

The book of Malachi has taught me that there is another mindset that can greatly diminish my devotion to the Lord. It occurs when I find myself disappointed with God. When I am discontent with the blessings that have been given to me from the gracious hand of the Lord, while demanding more of the blessing that God has granted to others. An attitude of disappointment with God can be the product of growing impatience with the Lord's timing and perceived lack of intervention into the difficult situations of my life.

We know that God's timing is perfect and that the outworking of His providence reflects the perfection of His knowledge and wisdom (cf. Ecclesiastes 3:11). But this wonderful truth seems to bring little comfort to those who are dealing with the daily discouragement of life's unpredictable calamities. This is what happened to the people of Israel during the days of the prophet Malachi. They were essentially disappointed with God, His provisions and His prophetic plan for Israel. This mind-set toward Jehovah took them to a place of spiritual corruption that not only impacted each of them personally, but also their families and their nation.

Someone has said that the most important thing you think is what you think about God, and that your thinking must be a reflection of God's self-disclosure found in His Word. The book of Malachi has taught me that equally important is your attitude toward God. Job serves as a great example of maintaining the proper mindset toward the Almighty, while your whole world seems to be crashing down around you (cf. Job 1). Habakkuk is an example of right thinking toward the Lord when you don't understand His plan (Habakkuk 2:17-19). Paul illustrates the attitude one should have toward our sovereign Lord while suffering unjust imprisonment (Philippians 1:12-18; 3:1; 4:4-13).

It is my prayerful desire that this book will cause us all to recalibrate our mindset toward God. This final book of the Old Testament warns us that great spiritual danger awaits those who have chosen a mind-set toward our Lord such as the one held by the majority of Israel during the ministry of Malachi. Our perspective toward the living Lord should always reflect the truth that we fear God and seek to bring Him glory in all that we do-- even when our circumstances change and His plan seems unclear to us.

Pastor Jerry Marshall

The Oracle of Malachi

The danger of being disappointed with God

THE ORACLE OF MALACHI

Chapter 1
Passive-Aggressive Children

I am always amazed that some people do not recognize the relevance of God's Word. Everything in the Word of God is perpetually practical and continuously applicable for every age. God's Word has something to say to us this day and every day. It speaks to every circumstance and every situation of life--even in the books of the Bible that we might perceive to be antiquated and disconnected from our high tech, highly educated postmodern contemporary world.

The book of Malachi for example will startle you with its direct connection to many today that are disappointed with God's timing and put off by His perceived indifference to their present calamities.

Yet, we can be confident that in the outworking of God's providence, His good purposes and perfect ambitions for those who know Him and love Him will become a present and perpetual reality (Romans 8:28).

I am not accustomed to using a lot of labels that come out of the lexicon of psychology to describe various personality disorders. Some of these labels are attention deficit disorder, attention deficit hyperactivity disorder, obsessive-compulsive, bi-polar or co-dependent.

I suppose my reluctance to use these characterizations is born out of my concern that we may be providing a euphemism for a problem that might be better dealt with a more direct approach. Instead of using labeling, we should call a problem exactly what

1

it is. If the problem is a lack of personal self-control, then let's describe it that way.

If it is a problem of being too self-absorbed, let's not give it a label; let's describe it for what it is. If the problem is outright disobedience, then instead of applying a label, let's seek to conform our lives to God's moral injunctions rather than finding solace in a euphemistic title that seems to lessen the sting of our personal responsibility for our disobedience.

How Do You Find the Will of God?

The will of God is not found through some feeling, inner voice, external situational guidance or other subjective experience.

The will of God is actually something very clearly revealed in Scripture.

Scripture describes the will of God as Godly guidelines for living, wisdom and morality—and those guidelines are found in the Bible.

Many of these issues are moral in nature and cannot be resolved by declaring them a disease and prescribing a medication. They require the transformation of the heart. Both the prophet Jeremiah and Jesus spoke of the sin-sick heart of man as being the true source of our sinful behavior (Jeremiah 17:9; Matthew 5:19-20). This requires recognition of our true spiritual condition and a willingness to repent, and line ourselves up with the will of God.

In spite of my reluctance in the use of these various labels, I must admit that I've come across one that I think is most appropriate for the people addressed by the prophet Malachi, and that is "passive-aggressive."

2

THE DANGER OF BEING DISAPPOINTED WITH GOD

This modern-day personality disorder could be legitimately used to describe the relational condition of God's chosen people with their Lord during the days of Malachi.

Someone who is described in this manner is marked by aggression, anger and displeasure manifested in an unassertive passive way--such as giving partial obedience to one who is in authority, or heartless compliance, procrastination, stubbornness or inefficiency. And this can be accompanied by attitudes of apathy, indifference or ambivalence.

It is sometimes exhibited by giving partial obedience to an authority. You're going do what the authority asks you to do, but your heart is not in what you are doing. The passive-aggressive condition is exhibited in procrastination, by putting off something that should be done in a timely fashion. It could also show up dressed in stubbornness and sullenness.

It's nothing more than showing your displeasure toward someone in a non-aggressive manner. But it's still there. It's still brewing. It's still a corrupting undercurrent in the relationship.

What is Worship?

Worship as described in the Bible is not just singing. In Malachi's day it was reading the Word, giving offerings, presenting sacrifices and more.

A simple definition of worship is those who belong to God responding in adoration, reverence and submission to God's written revelation of His character and deeds.

For today's Christian worship must be a way of life. It should involve every aspect of church life and every aspect of daily life. According to Romans 12:1-2, how you live your life should be an act of worship to God.

3

THE ORACLE OF MALACHI

And when I look at the nation of Israel in the time of Malachi, I see the personification of a group of "passive-aggressive" people.

What we see in the first few verses of Malachi, and, as a matter of fact, throughout Malachi, are the people of Israel demonstrating this sort of passive resistance to God because they have become skeptical of His promises. They even doubt the love of God and are beginning to question the benefits of serving the God of Abraham, Isaac and Jacob.

As a result, they are not--in the midst of this skepticism--turning their back on God completely. But, in a sort of unassertive, passive manner, they are giving less than their best to the Lord of glory. They are placing a limit on the level of their commitment to Him.

They aren't lovingly obeying all of the Lord's commands exactly as these commands have been given in the law. Instead, they are giving partial and imperfect compliance, which is a reflection of their attitude of disappointment with God.

> **A covenant is an agreement between two people. Covenants between God and Israel were established by God and had specific promises and demands.**

They're treating the Word of God like a cafeteria line. They're picking this, they're choosing to do this, they're partially obeying this and they're ignoring that.

Worship is such a significant part of a believer's life, but because the people in Malachi's day are skeptical about the promises of God, and doubt the love of God, they have become careless, indifferent and apathetic about worshipping the true and living God.

They have grown indifferent to the truth. The truth doesn't light a fire in them anymore. There is no spark. After all, how can they trust the truth revealed in God's Word when they are questioning whether He truly loves them and whether His promises are worthy of their confidence.

They have become disobedient to the covenant of God. They have even become faithless in their marriages and stingy in their offering. And all this is happening because they have become disenchanted with the promises of God and are displaying their displeasure with their circumstances and their situation in a passive-aggressive manner.

They have imagined they would be in a better place and they are not. And they want to know why. They are in essence saying, "What's up with you God?"

Now, in order to understand this we're going to have to dive into a little bit of the historical background of the book of Malachi.

This book was written anywhere from 433-424 BC, about 100 years after Cyrus issued the decree which permitted the Jews to return back to Judah—if they so desired. It was written around the same time as the books of Ezra and Nehemiah.

THE ORACLE OF MALACHI

The divinely imposed 70 year exile of Israel has come to an end. And just like God promised in His Word, Israel has now returned to the Promised Land.

The Old Testament Scriptures inform us that the nation of Israel, both the northern and the southern kingdoms, had been exiled from the Promised Land because of their blatant disobedience to God. The reasons were many and we see some of them recorded in Jeremiah 2. They had given their hearts completely to idolatry. They had ignored the covenant of God. They had not observed the Sabbaths. They had gotten involved in gross immorality and they were treating the poor unjustly.

Therefore God used two nations as His agents of judgment--the Assyrian nation and the Babylonians. These powerful enemies of the people of God came and took them from the Promised Land, the land they were given after God rescued them from slavery in Egypt. The land they'd conquered under the leadership of Joshua. But, in accordance with God's prophetic Word, because of their disobedience, both the northern and southern kingdoms were removed from the land of promise.

> ## The Exile and Cyrus' Decree
>
> Jeremiah 25: 1-11 contains God's warning to the Jews as to the results of their rebellion—70 years of exile.
>
> The book of Lamentations records the beginning of the exile.
>
> Ezra 1 tells us that, after 70 years of exile, the Lord stirred up the spirit of Cyrus, king of Persia, and caused him to issue a proclamation allowing any of God's people to return to Israel to rebuild the house of the Lord in Jerusalem.

6

THE DANGER OF BEING DISAPPOINTED WITH GOD

But because of God's grace and mercy, He told them there would be a day of restoration. There would be a time when they would be brought back to the Promised Land.
After 70 years of captivity, that day has now come.

Solomon's Temple, which was destroyed by Nebuchadnezzar during the Babylonian captivity, has been rebuilt. But as it was being rebuilt the people cried because that temple no longer had the splendor it once had. It no longer had that glory it had in the days when Solomon built it. And there is already a brewing dissatisfaction in the hearts of the people because things are not like they used to be.

The people are once again offering sacrifices. The priests are again serving as bridge builders between sinful man and a holy God--presenting sacrifices in the Temple. The people are familiar with the law of God once again.

But not all is well in the land.

In fact, a serious spiritual disease now plagues all of Israel. And the result of this spiritual disease is widespread unfaithfulness, which is affecting the people's worship in the Temple and their marital relationships in their homes.

You see, it had been over 2,000 years since the days of Abraham and the promise God made to him of a land—Israel-- and a people and a seed--a savior--through whom all the nations of the world would be blessed. And in spite of the Abrahamic covenant, the Davidic covenant and all the other covenants revealed by God to Israel, none of these glorious promises have yet been fulfilled in their ultimate sense.

7

THE ORACLE OF MALACHI

At this moment, the time of Malachi, Israel occupies less land that they did before their captivity. And this long anticipated Messiah—the promised seed of Abraham--who was to come and restore the glory of days of Israel is nowhere to be found.

Essentially, the people of Malachi's day are <u>expecting</u> to be living in the blessings of the Messianic age. After all, they think, isn't that what the prophets declared before our captivity?

You can easily imagine their thoughts:

"Sure, the prophesies were right about our forefathers--that they were engrossed in idolatry and God would judge them by sending them into captivity. But were the Scriptures right about the promise of a golden period of time in Israel's history when we would be brought back to the Promised Land and when Israel would live under the Messiah's rule?"

Instead of living under the rule of the Messiah, the people of Israel are still living under Persian dominance. Instead of victory in war and abundance in nature, they are experiencing poverty, drought and economic adversity.

Their current condition has led them to discouragement, disillusionment and doubt. They just can't get it together. They

> **Where Can I Read More?**
>
> The Abrahamic covenant can be found in Genesis 12:1-3
>
> The Davidic covenant can be found in 2 Samuel 7:8-17

understand the promises of God are the promises of God, but the promises don't seem to correspond with their present experience. Their present experience is incompatible with their understanding of the promised Messianic age that they expected to come right after their exile.

And so their reaction to God is a passive-aggressive one. They don't reject God outright. They don't turn their back on God completely. They give him half. They give him a quarter. They can't sing like we might sing, "All to Jesus I surrender." Instead they are thinking, "Oh no! I'm not going to do that because, quite frankly, I'm angry with God. I'm angry His promises have not been fulfilled as **I** understood He said they would--and within my time frame."

R.C. Sproul, in the 1997 New Geneva Study Bible, says of their condition, "Malachi's word confronts a people skeptical of the promises and therefore indifferent in their commitment to live in the light of those promises and to worship and serve the Lord with all their hearts."

And it was this sort of skeptical attitude that is causing them to raise a series of defensive questions in regard to God's revelation being given to them by the prophet Malachi.

God makes a statement, such as "I have loved you."

And they say—and I can almost hear the skepticism—"How have You loved us? How have You loved us?"

But don't miss this. The people in Malachi's time are no different than a believer today who is dissatisfied with his or her lot in life. We have believers today who are a little upset with God because, in their minds, things should be better. They read in Scripture that God loves them and they say--looking at their current circumstance--"How have you loved us?"

God also raises the issue of dishonoring Him. And what do the people say in return? What do the people say to the omnipotent, omniscient creator of the universe? They basically say, "How have we dishonored YOU?"

So then God raises the issue of them defiling His sacrifices and instead of believing God, they quickly run to their own defense and say, "How? What do you mean? How have we defiled you?"

They are no different than if we are dealing with our kids and we tell them, "Look, you've disobeyed me," and they say "How? How have we disobeyed you? I did what you said!"

You know what I mean by that? You tell your son to take out the garbage. And he grabs the garbage can, looks at you and gruffly says, "Okay!" And then he storms out the door, kicking the garbage can all the way towards the outside trash cans, and you say, "Hey, hey, cut it out!" And he says, with total attitude, "What? What's the problem? I'm 'obeying' you, aren't I?!?"

It's the old idea of complying, on the outside but not on the inside. It's half-hearted acts of obedience that betray the true condition of the heart. This is the kind of attitude the people in Malachi's day have.

But don't look at this and say, "Well, that was the people of Malachi's day." Look, there are many of us today that are having the same sort of struggle. Some of us are ignoring the blessings that we have received in Christ. We are ignoring the certainty of the love of God. The love God has placed upon us. And we're looking around and we're saying, "Well my lot in life is not what I thought it should be. How has God loved me?"

Chapter 2
How Have You Loved Us?

Look at Malachi 1:1.

> *The oracle of the Word of the Lord to Israel through Malachi.*

The book begins by describing this communication of God to Israel as an oracle--which is a prophetic speech, an utterance or a declaration. The Hebrew word that is translated *oracle* is *Massa'* which literally refers to a burden.

It is right to consider this letter as a burden. Because it's a grave responsibility that rests squarely on the shoulders of Malachi to accurately articulate what God has disclosed to him. It's a burden in the sense that he must communicate this heavenly message in the precise way he has received it. He doesn't have a right to editorialize what God has declared. His job is to proclaim, with precision, the revelation of God to the people of God.

This is not a happy message for the prophet to convey. This word to Israel is a heavy burden that must be carried and delivered to Israel. This oracle is of a threatening and foreboding nature.

Such a beginning indicates that the relationship with Israel and the God of Israel was not in good order.

What do we know about Malachi?

THE ORACLE OF MALACHI

The word Malachi means "my messenger," and there is no record of his ancestry in Scripture. For those reasons, some scholars have concluded that Malachi is not a proper name for a person--that instead this is a title. They believe Malachi is just some anonymous spokesperson for God, to whom God has given this assignment, this burden, to declare all of these things that are contained in the content of this letter.

I disagree. If that was the case, if the name Malachi was just a title, then this Word of the Lord would have come through some unnamed or anonymous messenger of God. This is not consistent with the pattern we see in Scripture.

If you look at the consistent pattern of the books of the Bible we categorize as Major and Minor Prophets, you will notice that every one of those books were communicated through a specific person. Not a title, or some unnamed person who occupied an office, but in every case it was a person that God has chosen to reveal that particular truth, at that particular time. I think that the consistency found throughout the Old Testament says much to us.

I am convinced that the book of Malachi is truly a communication that came from a person named Malachi to the people of Israel during his time.

All the other books name the author of each book in the introductory heading and if this was simply an unnamed messenger of God that would constitute a break in this pattern.

Also, if we dig into material outside of the Bible--which is not inspired or God-breathed revelation, but is useful to understand the historical details of the book of Malachi--Jewish tradition identifies Malachi as a member of the Great Synagogue that collected and preserved the Scriptures. So, Jewish tradition did not think that this prophet was some unnamed messenger of God. They saw him as a specific person.

As a matter of fact, the early church fathers said that Malachi was a Levite from the region of Zebulon--which would later be known as Lower Galilee. In fact, Nazareth was part of Zebulon, and Bethlehem sat less than 10 miles to the west of the region's western border.

So both Jewish tradition and the early church fathers believe that Malachi was a person. As do I.

This letter brings the Old Testament canon to a conclusion. With this last work in the Minor Prophets, God closes the Old Testament canon. From this day forward, there would be 400 years of silence. No communication from God to His people, other than what was already contained in the 39 books of the Old Testament.

Until one day!

One day, this man out in the wilderness began to yell, "Repent for the kingdom of God is at hand." This man was John the Baptist. And John heralded what some of us see as the beginning of a new era.

> The "canon" refers to the rule of the standards that a book or letter had to meet in order to be included in the inspired Word of God.

THE ORACLE OF MALACHI

Now, look at Malachi 1:2.

> *"I have loved you," says the Lord. But you say, "How have You loved us?" "Was not Esau Jacob's brother?" declares the Lord "Yet I have loved Jacob."*

God begins this oracle, or burden, with a straight forward declaration of His love for Israel. Now keep in mind, when this revelation is given the Israelite marriages are crumbling, they're breaking their marriage vows, they're not giving in accordance with the required giving of Israel as they should, they're giving animals that are less than perfect in the sacrifice and they're ignoring the truths of God.

And, 100 years ago, they returned from the 70 years of divinely-imposed exile. Still ringing in their memories is the horrific judgment of the captivity. And yet, they are now in a deplorable spiritual condition. It is quite easy to see that they are most unlovable at this time.

And yet what does God say in Malachi 1:2a?

> *"I have loved you," says the Lord.*

This goes deeper than a simple reflection on the past. If we look at the original Hebrew, the verb tense here should be understood as "I have always loved you." God is telling the unlovable people of Israel that He has consistently loved them. The Lord may have disciplined them because of their disobedience. He may have allowed the people of God to go through some tough times, but they should not assume that such experiences indicate that the Lord's love for His people has diminished or disappeared. For God declares, "I have loved you."

THE DANGER OF BEING DISAPPOINTED WITH GOD

The love of God for Israel is continuous in spite of the people's assessment of their current condition. God's statement, "I have loved you," indicates a long-standing, loyal love of unchanging commitment.

And what does Israel do in response to this incredible love?

They essentially respond with a challenge in Malachi 1:2b. They say to God Almighty, the Creator of heaven and earth, "Prove it! Prove it. You say You love us. Prove it to us!"

How have You loved us?

Now you might say, why are they asking that? This attitude is born out of the fact they have not yet seen the fulfillment of the Messianic Age to its furthest extent. They have not seen victory in war, and they have not seen the abundance of blessings in nature. Instead of living under the rule of the Messiah, they are still living under Persian dominance. Instead of victory in war and abundance in nature, they are experiencing poverty, drought and economic adversity.

They have not seen the fulfillment of the things God had promised in His Word. And they sort of demand, in their own hearts, that God fulfill His promises in their time--rather than His. Just 100 years ago, they had returned to the Promised Land after 70 years of captivity. But now, 100 years later, they have not seen the fulfillment of the promised days of the Messiah's millennial reign as promised them in Zechariah 14.

So, in light of these things, they are questioning the love of God, very directly. In other words, they look at their current condition and believe it is quite contrary to the claims of God.

THE ORACLE OF MALACHI

It's like dealing with a rebellious child, when after your declaration of undying love they respond by exclaiming, "How have you loved me? Prove it!" And that's essentially what's going on here, in Israel's reaction to God.

It's a challenge to the clear declaration of God's love. And it's no different than a believer today who questions the love of God--which is clearly revealed, clearly proven and clearly attested to in Scripture (see Romans 5:8, 1 John 4:9-10).

But the people of Israel are questioning the love of God because of their circumstance. They are asking, "If God really loves me, why is He letting me pass through this experience." They are saying, "If God really loves me why isn't He intervening, and why isn't He doing it now."

Amazingly, God condescends to answer their impudent question. I see this as another illustration of the manifestation of His patient love for them. He exhorts them to look for the evidence of His love by looking back, and then by looking around.

Let me say that again. He says, "Okay, you want evidence, LOOK back and then LOOK around." The first one is a challenge to look back to the past, and the second is a challenge to examine the present. He tells them to ask questions. "What's going on in the present? What's gone on in the past?"

God's response to their irreverence and impudence is to remind them of His sovereign love for them as the descendents of Jacob and His restoration of them from captivity--something He did not do for the descendants of Esau as seen in Malachi 1:2c-3a.

THE DANGER OF BEING DISAPPOINTED WITH GOD

[2] "Was not Esau Jacob's brother?" the Lord says. "Yet I have loved Jacob, [3] but Esau I have hated." (NIV)

Back in Genesis 25, Rebekah is told that these twins in her womb would become two nations. Jacob would become the father of the 12 tribes. Jacob would become Israel, and Esau would become the Edomites.

Esau and Jacob were the twin sons of Issac and Rebekah. They were the grandsons of Abraham. Esau was the older son, and he was the more favored son by Issac. And yet, in God's elective love, He chose Jacob to be the one through whom the promises He had given to Abraham would be fulfilled--including the promise of a Messiah. God would fulfill His covenant promises to Abraham through the descendants of Jacob, through the people of Israel, not the people of Edom.

Malachi 1:3, that starts with, *"but Esau I have hated,"* continues with, *"and I have turned his mountains into a wasteland and left his inheritance to the desert jackals." (NIV)*

According to J.F. Walvoord and R.B. Zuck, in their Bible Knowledge Commentary, both Israel and Edom received judgment from God at the hands of the Babylonians in the sixth century BC. Yet God repeatedly promised to restore Israel--because of His covenant promises in Deuteronomy 4:29-31 and 30:1-10--but He condemned Edom to complete destruction, never to be restored.

Israel has been restored to the Promised Land after the captivity and they are rebuilding their ruins. But this was not the case for the descendants of Esau, the Edomites. There will be no day of return or restoration for them.

17

Their land will be a wasteland forever and their inheritance will be turned over to the desert jackal--which is probably a reference to the Nabateans who ransacked Edom sometime between 550 and 400 BC and occupied their land.

God's love has made a difference in the fate of these two nations.

> *"God's love had made a difference in the fate of these two nations."*

History tells us, in the fifth century BC, the Nabateans, an Arabian tribe, occupy Edom--located south and east of Judea--and force the Edomites westward into a desert area later known as Idumea. In the fourth century BC, the Nabateans take over Idumea as well.

The severity of God's judgment on the descendants of Esau is because of their idolatry and their treatment of Judah when Judah was being defeated and taken captive by Nebuchadnezzar, as recorded in Obadiah 10-21.

Let's look at Malachi 1:4 for more details on the difference God's sovereign love makes for these nations.

> *Edom may say, "Though we have been crushed, we will rebuild the ruins." But this is what the Lord Almighty says: "They may build, but I will demolish. They will be called the Wicked Land, a people always under the wrath of the Lord." (NIV)*

The Edomites may declare in their haughtiness that they will rebuild their ruins, but such determination will never short-circuit God's sovereign judgment upon them. They may attempt to rebuild, but God will simply destroy what they do. Unlike Israel, Edom will always be under the wrath of God. For Edom there will never be a time of restoration.

The Apostle Paul reminded us, in Romans 9, that this choice of the younger son Jacob over the older son Esau was not based upon human merit. It was not based upon lovability. It was not because Jacob was more lovable and more alluring than Esau.

This love was rooted in the character of God and in the choice of God. It was not driven by human merit. It was not pulled out of God because He found these people to be lovable. It was simply God's choice of the people of Israel--and the placing of His affections on them. That's why they are loved. Because of God's sovereign electing love.

And it's the same for us. You can't earn God's favor. You can't be good enough to gain entrance into heaven. Your salvation, your forgiveness, is God's unearned gift to you. And all you can do is accept it. All you can do is realize you can do nothing to save yourself. And when you realize that, you throw yourself upon the mercy of God, give Him your entire life, submit to His Lordship, and you are saved from eternal punishment—and given eternal life.

The Elect?

The elect are those who have been sovereignly chosen by God to be His.

Look again at Romans Chapter 9. The Apostle Paul is trying to deal with the issue of why the majority of Jews in Paul's time are not turning to Jesus and recognizing Him as their Messiah. You can see the inference of the question--if Jesus is the Messiah then why aren't the Jews flocking to Jesus?

THE ORACLE OF MALACHI

Paul answers that question and he tells them, essentially, that not all descendants of Abraham are the true Israel (Romans 9:6). What he is saying here is there is a spiritual Israel and not all the descendents--the physical bloodline--of Abraham constitute the true Israel. And not all of the people are the children of God. Not all of them are a part the family of God.

They may be a physical descendant of Abraham, but they're not children of God in the spiritual family of God. And then Paul says, in verses 10-13 of chapter 9, that not all of them are God's elect.

Notice what he says in Romans 9:10-11a.

> [10] *And not only this, but there was Rebekah also, when she had conceived twins by one man, our father Isaac;* [11] *for though the twins were not yet born and had not done anything good or bad...*

You know what this means? There is a complete elimination of human merit. The election of God was not influenced by anything these unborn babies were going to do in life.

Romans 9:11 continues.

> *...so that God's purpose according to His choice would stand, not because of works but because of Him who calls...*

It is that effectual call which creates a desire and accomplishes what it commands. Romans 9:12-13 follows.

> [12] *It was said to her, "The older will serve the younger."* [13] *Just as it is written, "Jacob I loved, but Esau I hated."*

THE DANGER OF BEING DISAPPOINTED WITH GOD

And guess what Paul is quoting, part of Malachi 1:2-3.

> *² Yet I have loved Jacob, ³ but Esau I have hated. (NIV)*

Going back to Malachi then, what is God's answer to the people of Israel when they say, "How have you loved us?"

His answer is in essence, "I have loved you with free, sovereign, unconditional, electing love--that is how I have loved you. Listen, if it was because of your behavior, if it was because of the way you have demonstrated your lack of loyalty and devotion to Me, if My love was based upon the ever-fluctuating level of your commitment and your devotion, I would have fallen out of love with you a long time ago."

This is the essence of God's answer to them.

Later on in Malachi 3:6, God conveys a deep truth.

> *"For I, the Lord, do not change; therefore you, O sons of Jacob, are not consumed."*

What He is trying to convey to them is that it's not their ever fluctuating devotion, loyalty, professed love or worship that serves as the primary cause of God's love for them. God is saying, My love is a sovereign love. I was not constrained to love you. I was not forced to love you, I was not coerced. I was totally in charge when I set My affections on you. I have loved you, even though there is absolutely nothing in you to attract My love for you. We see this in Deuteronomy 7:7-8.

> *⁷ The Lord did not set His love on you nor choose you because you were more in number than any of the peoples, for you were the fewest of all peoples, ⁸ but*

because the Lord loved you and kept the oath which He swore to your forefathers, the Lord brought you out by a mighty hand and redeemed you from the house of slavery, from the hand of Pharaoh king of Egypt.

God is reminding them it's not because there was something special, something meritorious, or something notable about them.

God is saying, this love that I have for you is not because of you. It's because of Me and who I am. Not who you are. And not what you've done.

> **"The creator God, the owner God, the God who owns all things, has set His affections on you."**

Take a look at Deuteronomy 10:14.

Behold, to the Lord your God belong heaven and the highest heavens, the earth and all that is in it.

Do you know what that implicitly means? It means, God does not need anything. God is self sufficient. I would hate to attempt to be given the assignment to buy a gift for God because my God owns everything. He owns the heavens as well as the earth.

And then, Deuteronomy 10:15.

Yet on your fathers did the Lord set His affection to love them, and He chose their descendants after them, even you above all peoples, as it is this day.

Stand back and be in awe.

THE DANGER OF BEING DISAPPOINTED WITH GOD

The creator God, the owner God, the God who owns all things, has set His affections on you.

Amazing. Truly amazing.
Going back to the Malachi passage, let's speak to this issue of loving one and hating the other--as it is easy to misunderstand.

Specifically, let's read Malachi 1:2-3a.

> [2] "I have loved you," says the Lord. But you say, "How have You loved us?" "Was not Esau Jacob's brother?" declares the Lord, "Yet I have loved Jacob; [3] but I have hated Esau..."

What does He mean by this use of the words love and hate?
What do the words loved and hated convey in this text?

It's important to understand that both words are not referring to God's emotional reaction to the people of Israel and the Edomites.

These words are simply used to describe God's willful choice of one and His willful rejection of the other. They are descriptive of God's covenant relationship with Israel and the absence of such a relationship with the Edomites.

What is it that you and I could learn from this?

The lesson that we can take from this text is, the love of God for us is not to be measured by the favorable or unfavorable experiences we encounter in this sin-cursed earth. Rather, it should be measured by the truth that God has sovereignly chosen to place His love on us before the foundations of the world were established.

THE ORACLE OF MALACHI

There is no way for anyone to meritoriously secure the love of God. You know why? If you're born again, if you're part of the family of God, God's love has already been established and set upon you, as it is revealed in God's Word and proven by the giving of His Son. He proved His love for us by sending His only begotten Son to die in our place in order to reconcile us to God.

When I read the Scriptures, I know for a fact I am loved by God and I am secured in the love God has given to me, because it's not based on what I do. If it was, I'd lose that precious gift of the love of God. It's because of His sovereign choice, not because of my lovability.

Take a look at Ephesians 1:3.

> *Blessed be the God and Father of our Lord Jesus Christ, who has blessed us with every spiritual blessing in the heavenly places in Christ...*

Just as a side note, did you know those who are in Christ are complete in Christ? No one can add anything to what Christ has already given to me. Christ has given me every spiritual blessing and all that I need for life and godliness as seen in Colossians 2:9-10.

> *[9] For in Him all the fullness of Deity dwells in bodily form, [10] and in Him you have been made complete, and He is the head over all rule and authority;*

And 2 Peter 1:3.

> *seeing that His divine power has granted to us everything pertaining to life and godliness, through the*

true knowledge of Him who called us by His own glory and excellence.

Let's continue with Ephesians 1:4.

...just as He chose us in [Christ] before the foundation of the world, that we would be holy and blameless before [God the Father].

Now watch this, as we end verse 4 and move into verses 5 and 6.

In love, He predestined us...

Whose love? God's love! And you know what that tells us? It tells us His love was already in place.

⁴ In love, ⁵ He predestined us to adoption as sons through Jesus Christ to Himself, according to the kind intention of His will, ⁶ to the praise of the glory of His grace, which He freely bestowed on us in the Beloved.

And it goes on.

It's the love of God which compelled Him to choose you and me before the creation of the world. The love of God has already been placed on us. Do you understand that? Is your mind sufficiently blown yet?

Let me show you something else by looking in Ephesians 2:1-2.

¹ And you were dead in your trespasses and sins, ² in which you formerly walked according to the course of this world, according to the prince of the power of the air, of the spirit that is now working in the sons of disobedience.

He's describing all of us in our pre-conversion days. And verse 3 continues the thought.

Among them we too all formerly lived in the lusts of our flesh, indulging the desires of the flesh and of the mind, and were by nature children of wrath, even as the rest.

That is an unlovable condition. Not worthy of earning and securing the love of God. Ah, but note the next verses, verses 4 and 5.

[4] But God, being rich in mercy, because of His great love with which He loved us, [5] even when we were dead in our transgressions, made us alive together with Christ (by grace you have been saved)...

It is the love of God, manifested in His grace, which puts you where you into the family of God and makes you truly alive.

Take a look at what Paul said to the Thessalonican believers in 2 Thessalonians 2:13-15.

[13] But we should always give thanks to God for you..."

Why?

[13] But we should always give thanks to God for you, brethren beloved by the Lord, because God has chosen you from the beginning for salvation through sanctification by the Spirit and faith in the truth. [14] It was for this He called you through our gospel, that you

may gain the glory of our Lord Jesus Christ. [15] *So then, brethren, stand firm and hold to the traditions which you were taught, whether by word of mouth or by letter from us.*

So, are you a little disillusioned or a little disheartened? Are you kind of like a young person using headphones to ignore his or her parents? Have you turned your heart away from God's Word? Have you grown indifferent to God, His Word and His commands? Not rejecting Christ outright, but sort of in an unassertive way, demonstrating your displeasure with God and your lot in life.

If you are in that situation, can I challenge you?

Look back! Look back to that time before the creation of the world, when our God--who is love--placed His love upon you. It's there.

Don't measure whether His love is there by your current situation. Don't measure whether or not God loves you because of the ever-changing circumstances you encounter on this planet. Don't measure whether God loves you or not because you have felt the pressure of living in a sin-cursed world.

God loves you. And God has proven His love for you.

Scripture gives more detail in 1 John 4:10.

> *In this is love, not that we loved God, but that He loved us and sent His Son to be the propitiation for our sins.*

Christ was the satisfying sacrifice for our sins.

And we can't forget Romans 5:8.

> *But God demonstrates...*

You know what that means in the Greek? Demonstrated! Showed! Revealed!

> *But God demonstrates His own love toward us, in that while we were "so lovable"?*

No! It has nothing to do with our lovability.

> *...that while we were yet sinners, Christ died for us.*

<u>When we were sinners</u>, God loved us!

I don't need to question the love of God for me. I don't have to stand in defiance of God and say to Him, "when have you loved me?" I know what the answer is. Before the foundations of the earth God loved me. And God's love is consistent. And God's love is something I can count on. I'm sorry to say, I give Him plenty of reasons to not love me. But His love doesn't change. Now, the challenge, in a practical way for you and me, is in John 13:34.

"We tell the world that we are disciples of Christ by our love for one another."

A new commandment I give to you, that you love one another, even as I have loved you, that you also love one another.

Wow, God! You're kidding right?

Couldn't You just lower the standard a little?

THE DANGER OF BEING DISAPPOINTED WITH GOD

In the manner that You loved us!? You were willing to send Your Son, willing to surrender the best in order to accomplish our best? Willing to love us even when You don't get love in return? Even when people are not lovable you still love them? And you want us to love others in the body of Christ in the same manner?

Wow!

And the Lord says yes!

And we say, but Lord, you don't know these people like I do.

According to John 13:34-35, the world will know that we are disciples of Christ, not by the particular translation of the Bible that we have, not by the name that's on our street sign on the front of your church, but by our love for one another.

I was driving by some church recently and they had a neon sign that read "Bible Baptist, Pre-Tribulational, Pre-Millennial." I suppose they thought people would go "Aha, the true disciples of Christ dwell in this place."

You know what Jesus said? The unsaved world will know we are His disciples if they see our love for one another.

And how do we love one another?

Unconditionally.

How do we love one another?

Permanently.

THE ORACLE OF MALACHI

So, before we move on in to discover the final communication from God to the people of Malachi's time, which was prior to 400 years of silence that ended with the appearance of John the Baptist declaring the coming Christ, let me make sure a few things have hit home.

First, the motivation for God loving us comes entirely from the character of God and His sovereign choice. It is never initiated by human merit or our lovability.

Deuteronomy 7:7-8 records why God loved the people of Israel.

> [7] *The Lord did not set his affection on you and choose you because you were more numerous than other peoples, for you were the fewest of all peoples.* [8] *But it was because the Lord loved you and kept the oath he swore to your forefathers that he brought you out with a mighty hand and redeemed you from the land of slavery, from the power of Pharaoh king of Egypt. (NIV)*

And Deuteronomy 10:14-15.

> [14] *To the Lord your God belong the heavens, even the highest heavens, the earth and everything in it.* [15] *Yet the Lord set his affection on your forefathers and loved them, and he chose you, their descendants, above all the nations, as it is today. (NIV)*

The Apostle John also reminds us about God's love in 1 John 4:19.

> *We love Him because He first loved us. (NKJV)*

THE DANGER OF BEING DISAPPOINTED WITH GOD

Second, the existence of God's love for us is not to be measured by our ever-changing circumstances experienced in this fallen world.

John MacArthur writes in The MacArthur Study Bible, "No one should conclude that God does not love His people because He afflicted them, but rather He loves them because He elected them."

And third, the love of God for us should not be called into question because of our impatience with His timing in the fulfillment of His promises, or our disappointment with what God has allowed to occur in our lives in the outworking of His providence.

What is the current condition of your relationship with the Lord?

If God was to declare His love for you, how would you respond?

Would you demand that He prove it or would you simply, in humility, be astonished that the creator God has set His affections on you?

THE ORACLE OF MALACHI

Chapter 3
Giving Less Than Our Best

For a good part of my journey in Christ, I have wondered why some who are truly born again lose a high level of dedication and single-hearted commitment to our Lord with the passing of time.

I have known far too many believers who, at one time, demonstrated deep devotion to our Lord. Who demonstrated a contagious enthusiasm and an unwavering obedience to Christ and His Word. But currently they seem indifferent and distant in their relationship with Christ, His church and the purposes of the church.

They haven't abandoned the faith outright but it seems like they're just hanging on, going through the motions, and on occasion, trying—without success—to rekindle the spiritual fervor that once directed their lives with no success. They skip church services more than they did in the past and they miss much of the sweet, continuous fellowship of the saints.

> **What does it mean to be born again?**
>
> To be born again or regenerated refers to the impartation of divine life to your soul which was once dead in sin. This is done through the agency of the Holy Spirit. It is to be spiritually born into the family of God, by God. (John 1:12-13).
>
> It manifests itself in a new disposition toward God and His will. Without new birth in Christ, you will not see nor enter the kingdom of God. (John 3:1-5)

THE ORACLE OF MALACHI

What happened? Where did their spiritual vitality go?

I believe the answer is found in the book of Malachi.

The Israelites of Malachi's day, like some of us, have become skeptical of God's promises and are therefore apathetic in their commitment to live in light of those promises. They are also apathetic in their worship and in towards serving the Lord with all their hearts.

In their skepticism, they have become careless in their worship, indifferent to the truth, disobedient to the covenant, faithless in their marriages and stingy in their offerings.

As I said earlier, they have become passive-aggressive in terms of their relationship with the living Lord. They are showing their displeasure toward God and His commands in a sort of non-aggressive way by giving Him partial obedience or heartless compliance, and have complete indifference to what God requires of them.

In other words, they are doing some of what God requires of them but not with a willing heart and not with total dedication. And in some cases, they are completely disregarding what He has said.

Their present experience is incompatible with their understanding and expectations of God, His promises and even His love.

It is this same mind set today that cools our commitment, impedes our devotion and limits our service for the Lord--and quenches our appetite for His Word.

THE DANGER OF BEING DISAPPOINTED WITH GOD

In the previous chapter, we ended at Malachi 1:4, so let's pick up again at verse 5.

As you recall, God had just said he loves Jacob and hates Esau. You should also recall how this love and hate were based on nothing the person did, but completely on the sovereign will of God.

The result of God's previous choice was the restoration of Israel to the Promised Land, and the destruction of Edom, the descendents of Esau.

The severity of God's judgment on the descendants of Esau was based upon their idolatry and their treatment of Judah when they were being defeated and taken captive by Nebuchadnezzar, as recorded in Obadiah 10:21.

> *Because of violence to your brother Jacob, you will be covered with shame, and you will be cut off forever.*

For Edom there would never be a time of restoration.

And, in Malachi 1:5, God tells the people to look.

> *Your eyes will see this and you will say, "The Lord be magnified beyond the border of Israel!"*

God desires Israel to see they are under the hand of God's divine blessings and Edom is under a divine curse. This in turn will cause the Lord to be great or magnified beyond the borders of Israel.

The proof of God's love for them in spite of their current condition is His sovereign choice of them to be His people and

THE ORACLE OF MALACHI

His preservation of them--in contrast to the Edomites.

But here come more defensive questions.

The next defensive question is raised by those who should be the spiritual leaders and teachers of the Law of God in Israel. Their question is raised in response to God's declaration that they dishonored Him. Look at Malachi 1:6.

> *"A son honors his father, and a servant his master Then if I am a father, where is My honor? And if I am a master, where is My respect?" says the Lord of hosts to you, O priests who despise My name. But you say, "How have we despised Your name?"*

"How have we dishonored you?" they ask. "With a disrespectful attitude," is the answer.

At a minimum level, it is required for an ordered society which professes to live under the rule of God to have proper respect for those who possess functional authority within it. This is necessary for the well-being of social order. This is a part of the building blocks of society.

All of Israel understood that a son must honor his father and a servant his master. The need to honor one's parents is imperative and the fifth of God's Ten Commandments.

So God asks, "If I am a father, where is the honor due me? If I am a master, where is the respect due me?"

In other words, if this was the desired mind-set at a horizontal level should it not be even more so at a vertical level?

36

THE DANGER OF BEING DISAPPOINTED WITH GOD

God has chosen Israel as His son. In Exodus 4:23, the Lord told Moses to say to Pharaoh that Israel is God's firstborn son.

> *Let my son go, so he may worship me. (NIV)*

Also, in Hosea 11:1, God says it again.

> *When Israel was a child, I loved him, and out of Egypt I called my son. (NIV)*

And in addition to being God's son, God has also chosen Israel to be His servant as seen in Isaiah 41:8-10.

> [8] *But you, O Israel, my servant, Jacob, whom I have chosen, you descendants of Abraham my friend,* [9] *I took you from the ends of the earth; from its farthest corners I called you. I said, "You are my servant"; I have chosen you and have not rejected you.* [10] *So do not fear, for I am with you; do not be dismayed, for I am your God. I will strengthen you and help you; I will uphold you with my righteous right hand. (NIV)*

God is their father and their master because of God's sovereign choice of them. And the proper attitude toward one who holds such lofty positions is one of honor and respect.

In light of this fact, their attitude toward God should be one of reverence, awe, worship and deference. However this is not the case. And the sad thing is this disease of dishonor and disrespect was flowing from the priests in Israel--who are showing contempt for the name of the Lord with open disrespect and willful disobedience.

THE ORACLE OF MALACHI

Can you imagine that? Those who are supposed to be the bridge builders between sinful man and a holy God are dishonoring the name of the Lord!

They are verbally affirming God is their father and their rightful Lord, but are submitting in no area over which He has rightful authority. In effect, they are despising God's name.

They are wearing the clothing that identifies them as priest of the Most High God. They are reciting the appropriate prayers and performing the mandated rituals and sacrifices, but an omniscient God is exposing their mindset and their motives.

If this is the mindset of those who are to be the spiritual leaders in Israel, it is no wonder those under their leadership share the same corrupting attitude toward God.

And this attitude of disrespect is manifested in their defensive question. "How have we shown contempt for your name? What do you mean? How have we despised your name or acted in disrespect for who you are?"

Israel is showing quite clearly, your attitude toward God will manifest itself in the conduct of your life, the preeminent focus of your life and in your service of the Lord.

And in Malachi 1:7-9, the Lord keeps giving reasons.

> [7] "You are presenting defiled food upon My altar But you say, 'How have we defiled You?' In that you say, 'The table of the Lord is to be despised.' [8] But when you present the blind for sacrifice, is it not evil? And when you present the lame and sick, is it not evil? Why not offer it to your governor? Would he be pleased with

THE DANGER OF BEING DISAPPOINTED WITH GOD

you? Or would he receive you kindly?" says the Lord of hosts. [9] "But now will you not entreat God's favor, that He may be gracious to us? With such an offering on your part, will He receive any of you kindly?" says the Lord of hosts.

In spite of the clear instructions God has given to the priests of Israel about what is, and what is not, an acceptable sacrifice to bring to the altar of the Lord, they are ignoring these revealed regulations and are approaching God, on behalf of the people and themselves, on their own terms--bearing offerings that are far from acceptable and certainly not the best.

The defiled food being placed on the altar of the Lord is a manifestation of their attitude toward the service of the Lord-- which is a mindset of contempt.

Remember, this mindset is born out of their disillusion, doubt and disappointment with God and His promises--as well as their present circumstances.

Background Info

For more information and background on the regulations and guidelines surrounding Israel's sacrificial system, read Leviticus 22:17-25

And so, they are showing their contempt by offering blind, crippled and diseased animals to a Holy God. And God considers this to be an evil act. It is morally defiling and profoundly disrespectful to present such defective sacrifices to the Lord of the universe. It is in direct disobedience to God's regulations about what is, and what is not, a sacrifice that God would accept.

THE ORACLE OF MALACHI

This standard is also addressed in Deuteronomy 15:21.

> *If an animal has a defect, is lame or blind, or has any serious flaw, you must not sacrifice it to the Lord your God. (NIV)*

According to Dr. Warren Wiersbe, "Israel's law stated the lambs to be offered were to be perfect--unblemished--and yet here you have the spectacle of a flea bitten second-rate animal hobbling along on crutches. And the question in everybody's mind as they see it there is, 'Will it make it all the way to the altar?' In other words, the people are doing their best to offer a sacrifice that is no sacrifice at all. If you have a blind three-legged lamb, who's going to miss giving that to God? It's no sacrifice at all--but the priests were perfectly happy with it."

So, in Malachi 1:8, the Lord challenges them to try offering this stuff to their political master--most likely the Persian governor or his representative.

How do you think he would respond to such defective gifts? No doubt, there would be a swift consequence to such an act of dishonor.

Chances are, few would have the audacity to demean their leaders in such a way. Therefore, why would they offer such defective sacrifices to God?

Let's look at Malachi 1:9 again.

> *"But now will you not entreat God's favor, that He may be gracious to us? With such an offering on your part, will He receive any of you kindly?" says the Lord of hosts.*

THE DANGER OF BEING DISAPPOINTED WITH GOD

As they're presenting less then their best to God, at the same time they're imploring Him to be gracious to them. So, the Lord fires a very direct, rhetorical question at them.

> *"With such an offering on your part, will He receive any of you kindly?" says the Lord of hosts.*

Next God moves to Israel's worship. And in Malachi 1:10-14, He calls it despicable.

> *[10] "Oh that there were one among you who would shut the gates, that you might not uselessly kindle fire on My altar! I am not pleased with you," says the Lord of hosts, "nor will I accept an offering from you. [11] For from the rising of the sun even to its setting, My name will be great among the nations, and in every place incense is going to be offered to My name, and a grain offering that is pure; for My name will be great among the nations," says the Lord of hosts. [12] "But you are profaning it, in that you say, 'The table of the Lord is defiled, and as for its fruit, its food is to be despised.' [13] You also say, 'My, how tiresome it is!' And you disdainfully sniff at it," says the Lord of hosts, "and you bring what was taken by robbery and what is lame or sick; so you bring the offering! Should I receive that from your hand?" says the Lord. [14] "But cursed be the swindler who has a male in his flock and vows it, but sacrifices a blemished animal to the Lord, for I am a great King," says the Lord of hosts, "and My name is feared among the nations."*

God is crying out for just one lowly priest among them who breaks rank and declares in frustration, "That's enough! This is not right!" And slams the Temple doors shut thus keeping the others from lighting useless fires for unacceptable sacrifices.

At this point no worship at all would be preferable to the worthless worship taking place in the Temple. God says He'd prefer to be treated with outright hostility than with this parody of love and worship.

The Lord is interested in heart-felt honor not mere formalism or ritualism. Their worship of God is outward and insincere. So God would rather see it <u>all</u> stop.

The words in the second half of Malachi 1:10 are stunning words for those in the service of the Lord to hear from the Lord.

> *"I am not pleased with you," says the Lord Almighty,*
> *"and I will accept no offering from your hands." (NIV)*

But, in Malachi 1:11, the Lord looks ahead to a future time when everyone on earth will offer to Him the pure worship he deserves. Although no specific time is directly mentioned in this text, this verse is most likely referring to the future millennial rule of Christ when there will be universal worship of the Lord in every place.

That future model of worship should be their present pattern of worship. And it should be ours. The kind of worship we see revealed to us in the book of Revelation should be the pattern of worship for us today.

By contrast, the priests of Malachi's day are profaning the name of the Lord--treating the name of the Lord with irreverence.

According to J.F. Walvoord and R.B. Zuck in their Bible Knowledge Commentary, "In verses 7-8 the actions of the priests are condemned; here, in verses 10-14 their attitude is condemned."

Apparently, they know the sacrifices offered to the Lord are defiled and contemptible--but they seemingly hold the view it is such a burden to maintain the requirements of the law in regards to the sacrifices and offerings presented to the Lord.
Boring! Burdensome!

Therefore they don't care about the quality of what is being offered to God.

Because of their current passive-aggressive approach to their relationship with the Lord, they lack the "want to" to do it right. Their bridge building responsibility is a burden, a bore and a labor of duty rather than a labor of love.

So, in Malachi 1:14, God places a divine curse upon those who make a vow to give to the Lord an acceptable male from his flock of sheep but in the end, offer a second-rate blemished animal. This is not something someone does if they truly fear the Lord.

And we should pay attention, and examine our own lives. Do our lives and our relationship with God mirror those of the Israelites?

Are we going through the motions? Are we giving second best, or giving at all? If we find this is the case, we should go back to the basics and remember the motivation for God loving us comes entirely from the character of God and His sovereign choice. It is never initiated or secured by human merit or our lovability.

THE ORACLE OF MALACHI

Also, the love of God for us should not be called into question because of our impatience with God's timing in the fulfillment of His promises or our disappointment with what God has allowed in our lives in the outworking of His providence.

> **John 4:23-24**
>
> [23] But an hour is coming, and now is, when the true worshipers will worship the Father in spirit and truth; for such people the Father seeks to be His worshipers. [24] God is spirit, and those who worship Him must worship in spirit and truth.

We must avoid letting our disappointment, doubts and discouragements distort our view of God, and therefore rob us of our intimacy with God and cool our commitment to do His will.

And on Sundays, we must remember there is only one legitimate seeker in the church on a Sunday morning. It is God who seeks those who would worship Him in spirit and in truth as seen in John 4:23-24. To give Him anything less than our best is to profane His name.

Chapter 4
A Dishonorable Discharge

Mike Easley, the former president of Moody Bible Institute, wrote about his friend Lt. Col. Brian Birdwell, who suffered severe burns over most of his body as a result of the impact of American Airlines flight 77, when it was crashed into the Pentagon by terrorists on September 11, 2001.

While recovering from his injuries, President George W. Bush came to visit him and all the victims of this terrible tragedy.

Mike Easley writes, "According to military protocol, the junior soldier should salute his senior officer and hold the salute until it is returned. On that day, the Commander-in-Chief saluted Brian.

"Brian, in excruciating pain, struggled with all his might to return the gesture, and as he did, the president held his salute, tears welling up in his eyes, pouring courage into Brian with every passing second." The mutual expression of honor and respect had been exchanged.

The president honored this injured soldier for his service to his country. And Brian rightfully honored the president as his Commander-in-Chief.

What is consistently true, no matter the nature of a person's ministry, is the aim of their service must be to honor God, obey His Word, communicate His Word faithfully, given the opportunity, and serve others rather than themselves in the name of Christ.

THE ORACLE OF MALACHI

And those who would serve others in the name of the Lord must honor the Lord in the way they serve. In other words, you serve the Lord for His glory and you honor God in the way you serve.

This was not the case in the days of Malachi. Those who are the "bridge builders" between a Holy God and sinful man, the priests of Israel, are dishonoring God in the discharge of their priestly duties by carrying them out independent of God's standards and with an attitude of contempt for their calling.

This is the priest's passive-aggressive response to God and His standards. This is their non-aggressive way of demonstrating their displeasure with God and His promises.

Having issued a sound rebuke against the priests for their corrupt and sinful practices, the Lord issues a stern warning of pending judgment. This divine judgment will come upon the priests if they refuse to serve Him in the right manner and with the right mind-set.

In this warning, there are some practical insights for faithful service that all true believers need to know and need to apply, since every true believe has been called and equipped to serve the Lord and His purposes for the church.

The proof that every believer has been called into ministry is that they have been given spiritual gifts for ministry by the Holy Spirit.

Malachi 2:1-9 provides several insights for engaging in ministry that truly honors the Lord.

> *1 "And now this commandment is for you, O priests. 2 If you do not listen, and if you do not take it to heart to*

46

*give honor to My name," says the Lord of hosts, "then I
will send the curse upon you and I will curse your
blessings; and indeed, I have cursed them already,
because you are not taking it to heart. [3] Behold, I am
going to rebuke your offspring, and I will spread refuse
on your faces, the refuse of your feasts; and you will be
taken away with it. [4] Then you will know that I have sent
this commandment to you, that My covenant may
continue with Levi," says the Lord of hosts. [5] "My
covenant with him was one of life and peace, and I gave
them to him as an object of reverence; so he revered Me
and stood in awe of My name. [6] True instruction was in
his mouth and unrighteousness was not found on his
lips; he walked with Me in peace and uprightness, and
he turned many back from iniquity. [7] For the lips of a
priest should preserve knowledge, and men should seek
instruction from his mouth; for he is the messenger of
the Lord of hosts. [8] But as for you, you have turned aside
from the way; you have caused many to stumble by the
instruction; you have corrupted the covenant of Levi,"
says the Lord of hosts. [9] "So I also have made you
despised and abased before all the people, just as you
are not keeping My ways but are showing partiality in
the instruction."*

These insights will be unpacked for us as we examine the
Lord's admonition directed to the priests in Israel.

Their Mandate

Malachi 2 begins, verses 1-4, with a command or admonition
coming from God and directed toward the priests of Israel.

¹ "And now this commandment is for you, O priests. ² If you do not listen, and if you do not take it to heart to give honor to My name," says the Lord of hosts, "then I will send the curse upon you and I will curse your blessings; and indeed, I have cursed them already, because you are not taking it to heart. ³ Behold, I am going to rebuke your offspring, and I will spread refuse on your faces, the refuse of your feasts; and you will be taken away with it. ⁴ Then you will know that I have sent this commandment to you, that My covenant may continue with Levi," says the Lord of hosts.

Dig Deeper

Look at Hebrews 7:23-27, 9:11-14 and 10:11-18 for the Scripture presenting Jesus as our great high priest who was the ultimate sacrifice, who perfectly atoned for our sin, and who intercedes for us today.

The word "commandment" comes from the Hebrew word, *"mitsvaw"* which refers to that which is stated with force and authority--in this case, divine authority--and must be obeyed by those to whom it is directed.

Now, your reaction might be that you are "off the hook" in terms of this command. After all, the passage couldn't be more direct – it's directed to the priests of Israel during the time of Malachi.

Grab a Bible and start looking at these scriptures in the coming pages.

What relevance would this command have for the average believer in Jesus Christ today? After all, according to Hebrews 10:1-18, this type of priesthood came to an end.

And you would be correct. The office of the Old Testament priesthood did indeed come to an end when our great high priest, the Lord Jesus Christ, presented the ultimate sacrifice of Himself to be our sin bearer, and to perfectly atone for our sins once for all time, satisfying God's righteous judgment and ever living to make intercession for all true believers.

Currently, the New Testament offices of the church are the teaching office occupied by the elders, who are also called overseers and shepherds--as seen in Acts 20:28, 1 Timothy 3:1-7 and 1 Peter 5:1-4--and the serving office which is occupied by the deacons referenced in 1 Timothy 3:8-13.

But there is no New Testament office of priests whose duty is to serve as a mediator between God and sinful people. There is no one who is instructed to stand between God's righteous wrath and the people deserving judgment, offering atoning sacrifices in order to assuage God's wrath and to intercede for the people. No, Christ did this once, for all time! According to 1 Timothy 2:5, He is the only mediator between God and man.

That is why I never refer to our Sunday service as a mass, such as

---

Transubstantiation

The conversion of one thing into another.

In Roman Catholic theology it is the conversion of the bread and wine used during communion into the actual body and blood of Jesus Christ.

you would see in the Roman Catholic Church. In the theology of Roman Catholicism, they see the priesthood as being mediators and the mass as being a perpetual sacrifice.

As a result, the priesthood in the Roman Catholic Church is extremely important to them because they believe a real sacrifice is presented for the forgiveness of their sins during the mass.

In their observance of communion, they strongly believe that the bread and the cup are really transubstantiated into the body and blood of Christ and are offered up to God for the forgiveness of sins. But such a belief and practice stands in contrast to the once-for-all-time sacrifice of Christ on the cross which effectively put an end to any need for more sacrifices for the forgiveness of sins.

But the Apostle Peter, in 1 Peter 2:5, does describe every believer who makes up the church as a "Holy priesthood" in which we offer up to God spiritual sacrifices which are acceptable to God through Jesus Christ. And in 1 Peter 2:9, he describes all true believers as a royal priesthood. We are priests of the King of Kings.

The primary benefit of this New Testament priesthood is open access to God in prayer. We don't need a mediator to come to God in prayer in our hour of need. Christ, our great High Priest, has provided for us open access to the throne of God so that we might come in prayer at anytime.

We don't offer bloody sacrifices, but spiritual sacrifices--such as the presentation of ourselves in complete surrender to the purposes and will of the Lord, as seen in Romans 12:1-2.

THE DANGER OF BEING DISAPPOINTED WITH GOD

We offer up to God the sacrifice of praise and thanksgiving--as revealed in Hebrews 13:15--and the sacrifice of doing good for others by willingly sharing our resources--referenced in Hebrews 13:15b-16.

This is called the priesthood of believers--but it is not descriptive of an office as much as it is descriptive of our identity in Christ. It is the descriptive of the service of the saved.

But we will note that the command given to the priest of Malachi's day is equally applicable to all New Testament believers who compose the holy and royal priesthood referred to by the Apostle Peter.

Given the context of these nine verses, the nature of this command is that the priest of Israel must honor God or give Him glory in their service--as opposed to the dishonor that is described in chapter one--and to discharge their responsibilities as priest as they are stipulated in God's Word--as opposed to what they were currently doing.

And if they refuse to obey this command, a fourfold curse will come upon them and their descendants as God says in Malachi 2:2.

> *"If you do not listen, and if you do not take it to heart to give honor to My name," says the Lord of hosts, "then I will send the curse upon you and I will curse your blessings; and indeed, I have cursed them already, because you are not taking it to heart."*

Let's examine the exact meaning of the original Hebrew words used in this verse.

THE ORACLE OF MALACHI

"If you do not listen," is the Hebrew word *Shaw-mah*, which means to listen with the intent of yielding to God's command.

The phrase *"take it to heart"* refers to setting in one's heart as a primary life principle, the value of honoring the name of God in all that you do. It is essential to honor the name of the Lord because His name represents a summation of all that He is. The monogram of God speaks of His attributes, His reputation and His authoritative word.

God's name is serious business, and nothing pollutes it more than the misconduct of those whose business is to honor it.

The nature of the curse is to remove from them the divine blessings afforded to them because of their office and the blessings associated with such a respected position in the nation of Israel. If they disobey God and do not honor Him in the performance of their service, they will experience failure, disgrace and want. They will be cursed by God, which means that they will be the focus of the wrath and judgment of God.

In fact, the effect of God's judgment upon the priests of Israel had already begun because they did not take this matter of honoring God in their attitude and in their service to heart.

The oracle of God continues and is recorded for us in Malachi 2:3.

> *Behold, I am going to rebuke your offspring, and I will spread refuse on your faces, the refuse of your feasts; and you will be taken away with it.*

The word descendants in the NIV or offspring in the NASB can be understood either as one's offspring or as grain--seed used for planting crops. It is probably best to understand that God, in reaction to the perpetuation of dishonor and disrespect demonstrated by the priest of Malachi's day, would have to rebuke their descendants who would naturally emulate that attitude that they had witnessed from their fathers when they were serving the Lord in the Temple.

God would have to purge this generation of priests in order enable the next generation to serve Him and the people of God with dignity and honor.

God also declared that he will disgrace these priests if they continued to dishonor him in their service. And the nature of this disgrace will be as gross as the sin that makes it necessary.

God will spread on the faces of the priests' animal dung, and perhaps the entrails that remain after the priests' sacrifices.

And the priests with dung on their faces, will be carried away from the presence of the living Lord, along with the dung, the entrails and the hide of the sacrificial animals.

And the lesson learned from all of this is recorded in Malachi 2:4.

> *"Then you will know that I have sent this commandment to you, that My covenant may continue with Levi," says the Lord of hosts.*

They will understand that this command to honor God in their service does indeed come from God. And they will understand the covenant that God had made with Levi, the first priest of Israel, will not come to an end. Having cleansed the current generation of priests, God would make it so that He would not have to set aside the entire tribe.

Because the honor of the Lord is at stake, the quality of our ministries must never be mediocre or less than the best we are able to do by His grace.

We must minister not for the accolades of people but for the glory and honor of the name of the Lord.

The Model

In the second section of Malachi 2:1-9 God reminds them of the model He has given them.

Levi was the third son of Jacob by Leah and progenitor of the tribe of the Levites. Malachi uses the name Levi not so much to refer to the father of this tribe, but to his descendants who made up the priestly class in Israel.

This priestly assignment was given to them by way of a covenant with God which is articulated for us in Numbers 18:1-8 and 18:19-21. Salt is used metaphorically in these verses to describe the durability of this covenant with the tribe of Levi.

And, in Malachi 2:5-6, God reminds Israel of what He set up.

> *⁵ My covenant with him was one of life and peace, and I gave them to him as an object of reverence; so he revered Me and stood in awe of My name. ⁶ True instruction was in his mouth and unrighteousness was not found on his lips; he walked with Me in peace and uprightness, and he turned many back from iniquity.*

THE DANGER OF BEING DISAPPOINTED WITH GOD

Levi is used in this passage as a personification of the early Israelite priesthood. In this covenant with God, Levi would be given life and peace--both abundant life and tranquility of life as they served God faithfully. In turn, this priestly tribe was to fear the Lord and to stand in awe

> We must minister not for the accolades of people but for the glory and honor of the name of the Lord.

of the Lord's name--which is the whole point of this passage and the central aspect of the covenant.

This is absent in the generation of priests of Malachi's day. They need to go back to the original paradigm and covenant that God made with their tribe.

In the early Israelite priesthood this sense of reverence for God was manifested in what they did and who they were.

Literally in the original language, the first part of Malachi 2:6 could be translated, "The Law of truth was in his mouth and injustice was not found on his lips."

This should be understood to convey that not only did they serve people as mediators between sinful man and a holy God via the presentation of sacrifices; they also represented God by faithfully declaring to the Israelites the Law of God without partiality or deception.

And the characteristic conduct of the early priests of Israel--that is, their "Walk"--is described as one of peace with God--the absence of enmity with God--and is in conformity to God's righteous standards.

They were also God's agents of reconciliation, turning many back from inequity. They were using the Law of God to bring about repentance and correction in the lives of their fellow Israelites.

But this is not the model presented by the priesthood of Malachi's day. They do not give reverence God or His name and they are obviously not teaching their fellow Jews the Law of God. And instead of turning people from sin, they are modeling sin and disrespect for God and His Law.

Having been issued their mandate to honor God and having presented the model that they needed to emulate--which is the condition of priesthood in Israel in its early days, God, through Malachi His messenger, reminds them of their mission.

Their Mission

In addition to properly offering the sacrifices of the people to God, an essential responsibility of the priest was to guard, treasure, conserve or preserve on his lips, knowledge. That is, he must be ready to tap into his workable knowledge of God and His Law as revealed in His Word in order to give people guidance and instruction.

The priest, like all of Israel, was to preserve the knowledge of God and His Law from one generation to the next.

And the Israelites should be able in confidence to turn to the priest to get instructions from his mouth regarding God's law. Not to get from the priest <u>his</u> ideas, <u>his</u> wisdom, <u>his</u> insight, <u>his</u> perspective. No, they were to hear the Word of God from his mouth.

THE DANGER OF BEING DISAPPOINTED WITH GOD

For the priest was to be God's messenger. Not in the sense of a prophet who received new revelation, but of one who would accurately and carefully teach the revelation of God that had been received--such as was found in the first five books of the Bible. And the people of Israel should be able to rely on them for instruction from God's Word.

But the priests of Malachi's day are not being faithful to this mission. They certainly are not abiding by the Law of God in terms of the quality of the sacrifices they are offering to God. How can they be effective teachers of Law when they themselves are in disobedience to God's Law? Who would listen to them?

Their mandate is to honor and revere God and His name by serving God in accordance with His will. Their model is the holy condition of the early priests of Levi who served the Lord with honor and distinction. The Law of truth was in their mouths; they walked with God in peace and turned people back from injustice and sin.

Their mission is to preserve the knowledge of God and His law by communicating it from one generation to the next, to give guidance from the Law of God and to serve as God's messengers to Israel.

If they will not abide by God's requirement for faithful service, then God will dishonor them.

So, now we come to Malachi 2:8-9--their mortification.

THE ORACLE OF MALACHI

Their Mortification

> [8] *"But as for you, you have turned aside from the way; you have caused many to stumble by the instruction; you have corrupted the covenant of Levi," says the Lord of hosts.* [9] *"So I also have made you despised and abased before all the people, just as you are not keeping My ways but are showing partiality in the instruction."*

The priests of Malachi's day have departed from the proper way of conduct for those who are in the service of the Lord. This departure is not without its casualties; for they are the cause of many people stumbling spiritually by the perverted instructions they are giving to the people contrary to God's Law. They don't turn people from sin but rather cause them to stumble into sin.

They are in violation of the covenant that God had made with Levi. They are to honor God and revere his name and God in turn will bless their tribe. But they are not holding up their end of the covenant.

So God, in the outworking of His divine providence, is causing them to be mortified, humiliated and despised before all the people. If they will not honor God and revere His name, they will be dishonored before all the people.

Why? Because they are not following God's standards for functioning in their office and because they show partiality in their application of God's Law.

The chief end of the priest of Malachi's day is as it is of the Christian ministry and the Christian walk today--to honor God in all that we do.

THE DANGER OF BEING DISAPPOINTED WITH GOD

We are to bring Him glory by the conduct of our lives and by the quality of our service, as written in 1 Corinthians 10:31.

> *Whether, then, you eat or drink or whatever you do, do all to the glory of God.*

And Ephesians 3:20-21.

> *[20] Now to Him who is able to do far more abundantly beyond all that we ask or think, according to the power that works within us, [21] to Him be the glory in the church and in Christ Jesus to all generations forever and ever. Amen.*

And like the heart-touching honor exchanged between President Bush and Lt. Col. Brian Birdwell, God will honor those who would honor Him.

But we fail to honor God in ministry when we ignore His Word and attempt to establish the terms, the qualifications and the functions of ministry on the basis of some other source authority such as the mores of the culture, the traditions of men and desires of the congregation.

We are witnessing this in our day. There are denominations that ordain practicing homosexuals and place them into ruling offices in their denomination.

God is not honored in churches when His Word is ignored regarding those who should occupy the teaching and serving office in the church.

God is not honored when biblical doctrine proclaimed from a biblical context is ignored by those who are to preach and teach

God's Word. Unfortunately, the flock of God is not exposed to the whole counsel of God's Word. And the whole counsel of God's Word is the very thing they need for the nurturing of their souls.

As Dr. Walter Kaiser said, "It is all too easy to play to the gallery and give the pew what it thinks it needs (or to withhold what it thinks it doesn't need). But a true servant of the Lord proclaims and teaches the truth of God's word--all of it--whether or not it is popular or considered relevant by contemporary men."

Or how about John Piper who said, "One great danger to the pastoral ministry is that the voice of God in Scripture may be drowned out by other voices."

We fail to honor God in ministry and revere His name when we don't guard the truth, proclaim the truth and walk in truth.

All true believers are a holy priesthood and a royal priesthood. Do we honor God in the way we conduct our lives, our ministry and our commitment to God's Word?

Failure to honor God in ministry can have severe consequences. You need to only turn to some from our own day who know this truth. People like Jim Bakker, Jimmy Swaggart, Ted Haggard or the many priests who are serving time in jail for sexually molesting children.

Here we see another problem with having an attitude of disappointment with God. It's not that you stop serving God when you are embittered toward Him. However, your manner of serving Him and others in His name will be far less than your best. And in fact, you will dishonor Him by your heartless, mediocre activity ostensibly done in the name of the Lord.

THE ORACLE OF MALACHI

Chapter 5
Promise Breakers

Malachi underlines the truth that when our vertical relationship is out of order, our horizontal relationships tend to suffer. When things aren't right in an upward direction, our relationships with people often experience the consequences of our impaired fellowship with the Lord.

Certainly things are not right between the Israelites of Malachi's day and their God. From the prophecies of Isaiah, Jeremiah and others, Judah was anticipating a glorious restoration following their return from their Babylonian Captivity. However instead of "millennium blessings," they remain under Persian rule.

And now we move into Malachi 2:10-16, where we see that their disappointment with God leads to their disregard of two previously established commitments or vows.

Malachi begins by asking a couple of questions of Israel in Malachi 2:10a.

> *Do we not all have one father? Has not one God created us?*

An axiomatic truth in Israel is that God is the Father of all people because He is the Creator of all and everything that exists in the universe. However, God is the Father of the people of Israel in a very unique way. Of all the nations of the earth, God has chosen the people of Israel to be His children and serve Him and Him alone. He will be their God and they will be His people, as revealed in Deuteronomy 7:6-11 and Amos 3:2.

THE ORACLE OF MALACHI

Since all of Israel has the same covenant relationship with God as their Father and Creator--since they are all a part of God's family, Malachi asks in Malachi 2:10, why would they deal treacherously each against his brother so as to profane, or to violate the honor of, the covenant of their fathers.

> *Do we not all have one father? Has not one God created us? Why do we deal treacherously each against his brother so as to profane the covenant of our fathers?*

The implication of these questions is that if the chosen people of God have one Father who is their Creator, they should be one with each other, treating each other with the sort of love and respect that family members have for each other.

To *"break faith* or to *"deal treacherously"* comes from one Hebrew word, *bagad* which is used five times in this passage-- in verses 10, 11, 14, 15 and 16. It means to act contrary to a settled agreement. The word conveys the idea of deceitfully maneuvering out of a previously ratified agreement or promise, or to simply promise something only to deceitfully break your promise at some later time for some sort of personal convenience or advantage. It is a violation of one's word.

It is cheating or swindling those who took you at your word.

Let's look at the rest of this section to understand the full context of what Malachi is saying. Let's read Malachi 2:11-16.

> [11] *"Judah has dealt treacherously, and an abomination has been committed in Israel and in Jerusalem; for Judah has profaned the sanctuary of the Lord which He loves and has married the daughter of a foreign god.* [12] *As for the man who does this, may the Lord cut off*

from the tents of Jacob everyone who awakes and answers, or who presents an offering to the Lord of hosts. [13]This is another thing you do: you cover the altar of the Lord with tears, with weeping and with groaning, because He no longer regards the offering or accepts it with favor from your hand. [14]Yet you say, 'For what reason?' Because the Lord has been a witness between you and the wife of your youth, against whom you have dealt treacherously, though she is your companion and your wife by covenant. [15]But not one has done so who has a remnant of the Spirit. And what did that one do while he was seeking a godly offspring? Take heed then to your spirit, and let no one deal treacherously against the wife of your youth. [16]For I hate divorce," says the Lord, the God of Israel, "and him who covers his garment with wrong," says the Lord of hosts. "So take heed to your spirit that you do not deal treacherously."

The rest of the context indicates that the particular covenant that Malachi has in mind is the covenant that God made with their fathers on Mount Sinai when God gave them His Law. This passage indicates that they are breaking faith with one another by disobeying God's law as it pertains to mixed marriages and divorce.

For more background context on the law God gave Israel related to mixed marriages and divorce, read Exodus 34:10-17 and Deuteronomy 7:1-6.

God requires of His chosen people that they would not marry outside of the people of God because such mixed marriage would inevitability lead to unfaithfulness to God through the practice of idolatry and the pollution of the bloodline from which the Messiah was to come. In addition, God requires of Israel that they be a separated people and a holy nation-- separated from all the other pagan nations--and their love and loyalty would belong exclusively to the only true and living God.

Such unholy alliances would endanger and greatly impair their single-hearted devotion to God and His word and steal their hearts away into idolatry. The Apostle Paul stated a similar word of warning to the church in Corinth about being unequally yoked in 2 Corinthians 6:14-18.

> *[14] Do not be bound together with unbelievers; for what partnership have righteousness and lawlessness, or what fellowship has light with darkness? [15] Or what harmony has Christ with Belial, or what has a believer in common with an unbeliever? [16] Or what agreement has the temple of God with idols? For we are the temple of the living God; just as God said, "I will dwell in them and walk among them; and I will be their God, and they shall be My people.*
> *[17] Therefore, come out from their midst and be separate," says the Lord. "And do not touch what is unclean; And I will welcome you. [18] And I will be a father to you, and you shall be sons and daughters to Me," says the Lord Almighty.*

Malachi's questions in Malachi 2:10 lead to the beginning of the formal indictment in verse 11a.

> *Judah has broken faith. A detestable thing has been committed in Israel and in Jerusalem: (NIV)*

THE DANGER OF BEING DISAPPOINTED WITH GOD

The whole community is indicted because of what is being done by many within it. Malachi declares that Judah has "broken faith" or dealt treacherously, and an abomination has been committed in Israel and in Jerusalem. It continues in Malachi 2:11b.

> *Judah has profaned the sanctuary of the Lord which He loves and has married the daughter of a foreign god.*

Let's dig deeper. To desecrate or to profane the sanctuary means to cause dishonor or disrespect, to violate the honor of someone or something. The word sanctuary is a translation of the Hebrew word *qodesh* which can be translated Holiness, set apartness or sacred, or it can refer to a place that is to be holy, set apart or sacred.

According to The Bible Knowledge Commentary by Walvoord and Zuck, it is best to understand "the sanctuary of the Lord which He loves" not only as a reference to the Temple--but rather to the quality of distinctiveness or separateness that the Lord desires in Israel. The sanctuary of the Lord in this text is referring to the holiness of the chosen nation itself.

Some in Judah are violating the holiness of the nation, the unique feature of being set apart unto God like no other nation, by marrying the daughters of a foreign God.

Both Ezra and Nehemiah had dealt with this problem of idol worshippers as well as recorded in Ezra 9:1-15, Nehemiah 13:23-27 and 1 Kings 11:1-6.

It seems likely that the Israelite men to whom Malachi is ministering are divorcing their Israelite wives and running off with younger and more attractive Canaanite women. This would be an ancient version of what is called the mid-life crisis today. In both cases the prophet is telling Israelite men and women that if they marry someone who is not committed to their Lord, or if they divorce their mates, they are violating a covenant.

In direct violation of God's Law, they are intermarrying with women who are not a part of God's covenant community and who are idol worshippers--thus making all of Judah vulnerable once again to the same kind of punishment that was experienced by Israel and Judah about 170 years earlier when they were led into captivity by the Assyrians and the Babylonians as a part of God's divine judgment.

Let's continue with Malachi 2:12.

> *As for the man who does this, may the Lord cut off from the tents of Jacob everyone who awakes and answers, or who presents an offering to the Lord of hosts.*

Verse 12 is a very difficult verse to translate from the original language; however the central idea of the verse is very clear. Malachi issues a curse on the person who marries the daughter of a foreign god by declaring that the consequence of such action is that the offending party should be cut off.

According to Walvoord and Zuck in their Bible Knowledge Commentary, to be cut off from the tents of Jacob meant either that the man would die or that his line would cease and he would have no descendants in Israel.

Such a cutting off would then preserve the purity of God's covenant people.

THE DANGER OF BEING DISAPPOINTED WITH GOD

Then comes Malachi 2:13.

> *This is another thing you do: you cover the altar of the Lord with tears, with weeping and with groaning, because He no longer regards the offering or accepts it with favor from your hand.*

God has no regard for their offerings and bestows no favor upon them, so they are weeping and wailing--flooding the Lord's altar with tears in response to this situation.

> **Marriage is not a contract but a covenant.**

They, like so many people today, don't seem to remember what God had said to King Saul through the prophet and priest Samuel in 1 Samuel 15:22, *"To obey is better than sacrifice."*

God has little interest in religious functionalism. He is interested in the condition of the hearts of those who profess allegiance to Him and whether their professed love for Him is proven by their willing submission to His standards.

Since God knows the condition of their hearts and the disobedience that characterizes their lives, He does not look upon their offerings with regard or favor—as we see in the next verse, Malachi 2:14.

> *Yet you say, "For what reason?" Because the Lord has been a witness between you and the wife of your youth, against whom you have dealt treacherously, though she is your companion and your wife by covenant.*

Their hearts are so calloused by their sin, they find themselves perplexed by God's response to their offerings and they are asking why.

Malachi states that the cause of God's response to you is that He is acting as the witness between you and the wife of your youth; because you have broken faith, or dealt treacherously with her, even though she is your partner in life and the wife of your marriage covenant.

Not only are they marrying the daughters of a foreign God--idol worshippers--but they are divorcing their own legitimate Israelite wives to facilitate such unholy alliances. This is no doubt being done by the priests and by others in Judah who are simply following their example.

When our vertical relationship is out of order, our horizontal relationships tend to suffer.

And God, who witnessed their pledge when they married the wife of their youth, is now the witness for their wife of the fact that these men have broken the marriage covenant and they are dealing treacherously with their wives in order to marry these pagan women. They are acting contrary to a settled agreement to commit their devotion to their wives for all of their lives.

This reminds us of the truth that marriage is not a contract but a covenant. We need to understand Scripture speaks of marriage as a covenant relationship in many places, including Proverbs 2:12-17.

> *12 Wisdom will save you from the ways of wicked men, from men whose words are perverse, 13 who leave the straight paths to walk in dark ways, 14 who delight in*

doing wrong and rejoice in the perverseness of evil, [15] whose paths are crooked and who are devious in their ways. [16] It will save you also from the adulteress, from the wayward wife with her seductive words, [17] who has left the partner of her youth and ignored the covenant she made before God.

The Evangelical Dictionary of Theology defines a covenant as "a compact or agreement between two parties binding them mutually to undertakings on each other's behalf."

The marriage covenant is a mutually binding commitment in which the principals vow to faithfully fulfill their responsibilities in the context of marriage for the benefit of their mate and for the glory of the Lord.

While the marriage covenant is unilateral in its establishment, it is mutual, or two sided, in its accomplishment.

Wedding vows then are a verbal expression of each of the principal's commitment to their individual responsibilities in the marriage union.

Vows are entered voluntarily, but once made, they become binding in the sight of the Lord.

You do not promise what your <u>mate</u> will do to uphold the marriage. You promise what <u>you</u> will do in order to uphold your end of the marriage covenant. Your promise is not only to your wife, it is also a promise to the One who created marriage.

In our day, many people pledge in the presence of God and many witnesses to love their mate and to comfort, honor and to keep their mate in sickness and in health and to forsake all others, giving their complete devotion to their mate for all of their lives.

But the men that Malachi is addressing in this passage acted contrary to the marriage covenant they freely entered into and vowed to uphold--in order to serve their own interest so that they might marry pagan women.

Let's read Malachi 2:15.

> *But not one has done so who has a remnant of the Spirit. And what did that one do while he was seeking a godly offspring? Take heed then to your spirit, and let no one deal treacherously against the wife of your youth.*

Verse 15 of Malachi chapter 2 is perhaps one of the most difficult passages to translate. I believe the NIV has done the best that you can do.

> *Has not the Lord made them one? In flesh and spirit they are his. And why one? Because he was seeking godly offspring. So guard yourself in your spirit, and do not break faith with the wife of your youth. (NIV)*

The first part of the verse takes us back to Genesis 2:24 when, shortly after God created Eve for Adam, He looked ahead to all future marriage relationships and gave us his blueprint for marriage.

> *For this reason a man will leave his father and mother and be united to his wife, and they will become one flesh. (NIV)*

THE DANGER OF BEING DISAPPOINTED WITH GOD

God desires that one man and one woman would enter into marriage for one lifetime.

Even though God had the power to make many wives for Adam He made only one wife for him. Why? Because He was seeking a godly seed; He wanted to carry on a godly remnant.

Polygamy and divorce are not conducive to nurturing children in the fear of God. Certainly, divorcing your wife in order to marry the daughter of a foreign god is not conducive to raising children who love the Lord.

And so God declares to Judah through the prophet Malachi, do not break faith with the wife of your youth--do not act treacherously against your wife. After she has given you the best years of her life, raised your children and served you as her husband--it isn't right for you to deal with her in such a deceitful manner and it is certainly against God and His intention for marriage.

Malachi 2:16 continues God's thoughts on the matter.

> *"For I hate divorce," says the Lord, the God of Israel, "and him who covers his garment with wrong," says the Lord of hosts. "So take heed to your spirit that you do not deal treacherously."*

Often in Scriptures it is stated that God hates or despises sin but in this passage you have God Himself declaring in no uncertain terms his hatred of two specific sins. God says, "I hate divorce"--literally the putting away. And God hates a man covering himself with wrong--which could also be translated violence, cruelty and injustice--as he covers himself with his garment.

THE ORACLE OF MALACHI

Because of the strength and clarity of God's attitude toward divorce, I am always suspicious of someone who tells me that they feel that God is leading them to divorce their mate.

God would never lead them into something that he has declared that He hates!

God in His mercy has given us some exceptions, but not the "50 ways to leave your woman" offer made by the legal system of our country. In our legal system, we have even provided no fault divorce.

What a misnomer. Every divorce involves fault. Chances are that both parties are at fault although God recognizes that some people might be victimized by hard-hearted, perpetual marriage covenant breakers. Jesus acknowledged in Matthew 19:3-12 that a woman may be the victim of a hard-hearted covenant breaker and divorce may be the sad necessity when your partner refuses to stop his or her unfaithfulness.

In 1 Corinthians 7:15, the apostle Paul also suggested another possible but rare scenario, when a believer is deserted by an unbelieving spouse because of his or her relationship with the Lord.

> **God would never lead them into something that He hates!**

> *But if the unbeliever leaves, let him do so. A believing man or woman is not bound in such circumstances; God has called us to live in peace. (NIV)*

So what does this look like today? How should we take these truths and apply them to our lives.

THE DANGER OF BEING DISAPPOINTED WITH GOD

I would suggest remembering some key points as you live out your life, and working hard to make them your lifestyle.

Always remember the strength and well-being of your marriage relationship is dependent upon the strength and well being of your personal relationship with the Lord. Your focus should first be on God, and then the fruit of your personal growth in your relationship with God should be applied to your marriage.

"But doesn't God want me to be happy?"

I have had many people ask me that question. The truth is, God has a greater value for the holiness of our lives and our faithfulness to our vows than our subjective perception of happiness. Although God has graciously provided a few exceptions for divorce, His attitude toward divorce remains constant because it always involves sin.

Also realize, the lower your view of God and the more exaggerated your view of self, the more meaningful relationships suffer. Damaging your relationship with God and God's people is never worth a spiritually destructive relationship with any person, no matter the intensity of your emotional or physical attraction to them.

Divorce not only breaks a particular social bond but, if it becomes widespread, it can undermine the fabric of other important social institutions of a society. In our culture, divorce and the destruction of marriage and the family will lead to cultural suicide unless we change our hearts and minds about this first and most important institution that was created by God.

THE ORACLE OF MALACHI

Chapter 6
Where is the God of Justice?

"It's unfair!"

What parent hasn't heard their children decry the perceived injustice of mom or dad's distribution of a special treat, privilege or a decision regarding punishment for some misbehavior?

"Your punishment isn't fair, it's too hard, it's not right," they exclaim.

It is within the fiber of our being to have a low tolerance for, and a high sensitivity to, any real or perceived injustice done to us. Some adults have been known to complain that the local police department has established speed traps on certain streets just so that they might meet a certain monthly quota of traffic tickets. They tell you it's not fair, but never consider that if you keep the speed limit you render the speed trap ineffective.

Recently, I heard that a judge from the U.S. Court of Appeals for the Ninth Circuit was going to let a convicted murderer off because his lawyer said that during the trial the relatives of the victim were wearing t-shirts displaying the picture of the victim. The lawyer claimed this unduly influenced the jury's decision. The judge agreed and ordered a retrial of this case which is over 10 years old.

Will perfect justice ever be experienced on this sin-cursed earth? Not until the perfect judge of the world comes to right all wrongs.

THE ORACLE OF MALACHI

Malachi speaks of the truth of the Second Coming of the Lord in judgment in order to deal with what some in Israel are saying about the justice of God.

The people of Israel are essentially exclaiming "It isn't fair. Evildoers are prospering materially. The wicked seem to be getting richer. God seems to be pleased with those who do evil. By contrast, those who are the followers of Yahweh are not blessed in this way."

"Where is the God of justice," they wonder.

Malachi's response shows that such a mindset toward God is unfair, unjust and without any merit.

Let's read Malachi 2:17-3:6.

> *2:17You have wearied the Lord with your words. Yet you say, "How have we wearied Him?" In that you say, "Everyone who does evil is good in the sight of the Lord, and He delights in them," or, "Where is the God of justice?" 3:1"Behold, I am going to send My messenger, and he will clear the way before Me And the Lord, whom you seek, will suddenly come to His temple; and the messenger of the covenant, in whom you delight, behold, He is coming," says the Lord of hosts. 2But who can endure the day of His coming? And who can stand when He appears? For He is like a refiner's fire and like fullers' soap. 3He will sit as a smelter and purifier of silver, and He will purify the sons of Levi and refine them like gold and silver, so that they*

In the midst of such experiences, it is not uncommon for people to wonder if God is just or if God really cares.

may present to the Lord offerings in righteousness.
⁴Then the offering of Judah and Jerusalem will be
pleasing to the Lord as in the days of old and as in
former years. ⁵Then I will draw near to you for
judgment; and I will be a swift witness against the
sorcerers and against the adulterers and against those
who swear falsely, and against those who oppress the
wage earner in his wages, the widow and the orphan,
and those who turn aside the alien and do not fear Me,"
says the Lord of hosts. ⁶"For I, the Lord do not change;
therefore you, O sons of Jacob, are not consumed."

Those who are most likely to question whether God is just are
those who have passed through some dark and difficult days
and who imagine that a just and sovereign God would not allow
them to experience such pain and suffering.

Perhaps they have recently experienced the death of a loved one
or the prolonged sickness of a family member with the
perpetual aggravation of not being able to do anything about
it. Perhaps they have just experienced a large financial
setback or the loss of a job. Or maybe they have been deserted
by their mate.

In the midst of such experiences, it is not uncommon for people to
wonder if God is just or if God really cares. From the context
of a hurting heart pulsating in

What is Idolatry?

In short, the proper Jewish definition of idolatry is to do an act of worship toward any created thing, to believe that a particular created thing is an independent power, or to make something a mediator between ourselves and the Almighty.

THE ORACLE OF MALACHI

pain, they take up their pen to write a new theology--a new perspective of God.

Surly God can't be just, loving, caring and sovereign. Where is the God of justice?

In their cynicism, the post-exilic Israelite remnant--now back in the Promised Land during the days of Malachi--has already questioned God's love, majesty and fidelity. Now they raise the issue of His justice. They ask, in a cynical manner, "Where is the justice of God?"

They think God is unjust in withholding what they consider their proper measure of material blessings. Even worse, they accuse God of favoring evildoers. After all, they see the Persians, who still rule over them, prospering. The evil Persians seem to be flourishing--but not God's people!

Their disappointment with God and His promises leads to a skepticism that causes them to question the very integrity of God's character.

They illustrate the principle that when we formulate our ideas of God, His character and His ways in response to the perplexing circumstances and other calamities of life, we will in the end deny the truth that our God does not change, and we will be thinking of him in ways that amount to idolatry.

A.W. Tozer, in his classic book, "Knowledge of The Holy," made the point that idolatry begins in the mind, when we think thoughts about God that are contrary to the revelation of God in the Scriptures.

THE DANGER OF BEING DISAPPOINTED WITH GOD

"Among the sins to which the human heart is prone," Tozer writes, "hardly any other is more hateful to God than idolatry, for idolatry is at bottom a libel on His character. The idolatrous heart assumes that God is other than He is--in itself a monstrous sin--and substitutes for the true God one made after its own likeness...Wrong ideas about God are not only the fountain from which the polluted waters of idolatry flow; they are themselves idolatrous. The idolater simply imagines things about God and acts as if they were true."

Malachi, under divine inspiration, answers their question regarding the justice of God although it is not the answer they expect. He informs them that God's justice will be fully expressed at the time of the Second-Coming of the Lord.

There are four informative points that Malachi gives in this section in which he will effectively deal with their question about the justice of God.

First, in Malachi 2:17, Malachi indicts his audience for wearying the Lord with their words or comments.

> *You have wearied the Lord with your words. Yet you say, "How have we wearied Him?" In that you say, "Everyone who does evil is good in the sight of the Lord, and He delights in them," or, "Where is the God of justice?"*

In other words they have tried the patience of the Lord to the point of exhaustion. Seven times in this book God makes a statement either directly or indirectly critical of the people and they reply by challenging the statement.

THE ORACLE OF MALACHI

If you remember Malachi 1:1-5 you will recall they question God's very direct statement of love for them when they said, "How has God loved us?"

They have also presumed upon the patience of God when the priest denied any impropriety in the discharge of their duties and asked indignantly, in Malachi 1:6-14, "How have we shown contempt for your name?"

They have the audacity to ask such a question while at the same time presenting to God blind and blemished sacrifices, offering Him less honor than accorded to their Persian governor.

They despise the table of the Lord, but will not admit it. Their worship is mere formality without heart, without passion and without real sacrifice.

They flood the Lord's altar with tears and want to know why God does not bless them in response to the sacrifices they have presented--while at the same time living contrary to the covenant of their fathers by marrying the daughters of a foreign god and breaking their marriage covenant with the wives of their youth in order to facilitate their passions for these pagan women.

But now in Malachi 2:17, they push the patience of God to the point of exhaustion by questioning the moral government of God, the holiness of God and the justice of God.

They are sarcastically implying that God must love wicked people because they sure seem to be prospering in this world. He seems to reward the wicked with good while withholding prosperity and blessing from the righteous.

THE DANGER OF BEING DISAPPOINTED WITH GOD

They think God does not discriminate between evil and good, and that He even delights in those who do evil. Therefore, they ask, "Where is the God of justice?"

At least five different biblical writers raised this issue of the prosperity of the wicked in light of the suffering of the righteous on this earth. Read Job 21:7-26.

> [7]*Why do the wicked still live, continue on, also become very powerful?* [8]*Their descendants are established with them in their sight, and their offspring before their eyes,* [9]*their houses are safe from fear, and the rod of God is not on them.* [10]*His ox mates without fail; his cow calves and does not abort.* [11]*They send forth their little ones like the flock, and their children skip about.* [12]*They sing to the timbrel and harp, and rejoice at the sound of the flute.* [13]*They spend their days in prosperity, and suddenly they go down to Sheol.* [14]*They say to God, "Depart from us! We do not even desire the knowledge of Your ways.* [15]*Who is the Almighty, that we should serve Him, and what would we gain if we entreat Him?"* [16]*Behold, their prosperity is not in their hand; the counsel of the wicked is far from me.* [17]*How often is the lamp of the wicked put out, or does their calamity fall on them? Does God apportion destruction in His anger?* [18]*Are they as straw before the wind, and like chaff which the storm carries away?* [19]*You say, "God stores away a man's iniquity for his sons." Let God repay him so that he may know it.* [20]*Let his own eyes see his decay, and let him drink of the wrath of the Almighty.* [21]*For what does he care for his household after him, when the number of his months is cut off?* [22]*Can anyone teach God knowledge, in that He judges those on high?* [23]*One dies in his full strength, being wholly at ease and satisfied;*

[24]His sides are filled out with fat, and the marrow of his bones is moist, [25]while another dies with a bitter soul, never even tasting anything good. [26]Together they lie down in the dust, and worms cover them.

And Psalm 73 for some of those examples.

[1]Surely God is good to Israel, to those who are pure in heart! [2]But as for me, my feet came close to stumbling, my steps had almost slipped. [3]For I was envious of the arrogant as I saw the prosperity of the wicked. [4]For there are no pains in their death, and their body is fat. [5]They are not in trouble as other men, nor are they plagued like mankind. [6]Therefore pride is their necklace; the garment of violence covers them. [7]Their eye bulges from fatness; the imaginations of their heart run riot. [8]They mock and wickedly speak of oppression; they speak from on high. [9]They have set their mouth against the heavens, and their tongue parades through the earth. [10]Therefore his people return to this place, and waters of abundance are drunk by them. [11]They say, "How does God know? And is there knowledge with the Most High?" [12]Behold, these are the wicked; and always at ease, they have increased in wealth. [13]Surely in vain I have kept my heart pure and washed my hands in innocence; [14]for I have been stricken all day long and chastened every morning. [15]If I had said, "I will speak thus," behold, I would have betrayed the generation of Your children. [16]When I pondered to understand this, it was troublesome in my sight [17]until I came into the sanctuary of God; then I perceived their end. [18]Surely You set them in slippery places; You cast them down to destruction. [19]How they are destroyed in a moment! They are utterly swept away by sudden terrors! [20]Like a

dream when one awakes, O Lord, when aroused, You will despise their form. [21]When my heart was embittered and I was pierced within, [22]then I was senseless and ignorant; I was like a beast before You. [23]Nevertheless I am continually with You; You have taken hold of my right hand. [24]With Your counsel You will guide me, and afterward receive me to glory. [25]Whom have I in heaven but You? And besides You, I desire nothing on earth. [26]My flesh and my heart may fail, but God is the strength of my heart and my portion forever. [27]For, behold, those who are far from You will perish; You have destroyed all those who are unfaithful to You. [28]But as for me, the nearness of God is my good; I have made the Lord God my refuge, that I may tell of all Your works.

We must not view God on the basis of our present circumstances but rather we should measure the present in light of God's eternal purpose for those who are His.

According to P.C. Craigie, in Twelve Prophets: Volume 2, the Jews of Malachi's day have become--by their attitudes and actions--functional atheists. Not bothering to deny the existence of God, but destroying any link between God and justice, or between the Almighty and good and evil.

Yahweh graciously answers their complaint in the opening verses of the succeeding chapter by showing that one is coming who will indeed right all wrongs—including those in the priesthood and the people of Israel!

But before that occurs, he will be preceded by the coming of the messenger of the Lord. This is Malachi's second point—and it is found in Malachi 3:1.

THE ORACLE OF MALACHI

> *"Behold, I am going to send My messenger, and he will clear the way before Me And the Lord, whom you seek, will suddenly come to His temple; and the messenger of the covenant, in whom you delight, behold, He is coming," says the Lord of hosts.*

It was quite customary in those days to send messengers in advance of a visiting king--first to announce his coming and secondly to remove any impediments to his visit. The Lord declares that He will send His messenger to come in a preparatory role.

The word translated *messenger* comes from the Hebrew word *"Malak"* which means my messenger and is the proper name of the prophet who was declaring God's Word to Israel at this time.

But Malachi is not the coming messenger. This messenger would be the one who would prepare the way for the coming Messiah.

Isaiah the prophet spoke of this messenger of preparation in Isaiah 40:3.

> *A voice of one calling: "In the desert prepare the way for the Lord; make straight in the wilderness a highway for our God." (NIV)*

The New Testament, in Matthew 3:1-3, identifies John the Baptist as the one who played this preparatory role.

> *[1]Now in those days John the Baptist came, preaching in the wilderness of Judea, saying, [2]"Repent, for the kingdom of heaven is at hand." [3]For this is the one*

referred to by Isaiah the prophet when he said, "The voice of one crying in the wilderness, 'make ready the way of the Lord, make His paths straight!'"

John would prepare the people of Israel morally by boldly confronting their sinfulness and challenging them to repent of their sins. And by pointing them to the Lamb of God who would take away the sins of the world as recorded in Mark 1:1-8.

[1]The beginning of the gospel of Jesus Christ, the Son of God. [2]As it is written in Isaiah the prophet: "Behold, I send My messenger ahead of You, who will prepare Your way; [3]The voice of one crying in the wilderness, 'make ready the way of the Lord, make His paths straight.'" [4]John the Baptist appeared in the wilderness preaching a baptism of repentance for the forgiveness of sins. [5]And all the country of Judea was going out to him, and all the people of Jerusalem; and they were being baptized by him in the Jordan River, confessing their sins. [6]John was clothed with camel's hair and wore a leather belt around his waist, and his diet was locusts and wild honey. [7]And he was preaching, and saying, "After me One is coming who is mightier than I, and I am not fit to stoop down and untie the thong of His sandals. [8]I baptized you with water; but He will baptize you with the Holy Spirit."

Jesus Himself clearly identified the messenger of Malachi 3:1 as John the Baptist in Matthew 11:7-10.

[7]As these men were going away, Jesus began to speak to the crowds about John, "What did you go out into the wilderness to see? A reed shaken by the wind? [8]But what

*did you go out to see? A man dressed in soft clothing?
Those who wear soft clothing are in kings' palaces! ⁹But
what did you go out to see? A prophet? Yes, I tell you,
and one who is more than a prophet. ¹⁰This is the one
about whom it is written, 'Behold, I send My messenger
ahead of You, who will prepare Your way before You.'"*

The Jews of Jesus' time expected that a resurrected Elijah
would precede the coming of the Messiah. We know this
because a little further on, in Malachi 4:5, the Prophet Malachi
declares, *"Behold, I am going to send you Elijah the prophet
before the coming of the great and terrible day of the Lord."*

Jesus said that John the Baptist is the Elijah who was to come in
Matthew 11:14.

*And if you are willing to accept it, John himself is Elijah
who was to come.*

Luke 1:11-17 tells us the Angel of the Lord who announced
John's birth to his father Zechariah, declared that John would
prepare the way of the Lord in the spirit of Elijah.

*¹¹And an angel of the Lord appeared to him, standing to
the right of the altar of incense. ¹²Zacharias was
troubled when he saw the angel, and fear gripped him.
¹³But the angel said to him, "Do not be afraid,
Zacharias, for your petition has been heard, and your
wife Elizabeth will bear you a son, and you will give him
the name John. ¹⁴You will have joy and gladness, and
many will rejoice at his birth. ¹⁵For he will be great in
the sight of the Lord; and he will drink no wine or
liquor, and he will be filled with the Holy Spirit while
yet in his mother's womb. ¹⁶And he will turn many of the*

sons of Israel back to the Lord their God. [17]It is he who will go as a forerunner before Him in the spirit and power of Elijah, to turn the hearts of the fathers back to the children, and the disobedient to the attitude of the righteous, so as to make ready a people prepared for the Lord."

And John denied that he was the actual Elijah resurrected but he did acknowledge that he is the one that Isaiah the prophet spoke of--in John 1:19-27.

[19]This is the testimony of John, when the Jews sent to him priests and Levites from Jerusalem to ask him, "Who are you?" [20]And he confessed and did not deny, but confessed, "I am not the Christ." [21]They asked him, "What then? Are you Elijah?" And he said, "I am not." "Are you the Prophet?" And he answered, "No." [22]Then they said to him, "Who are you, so that we may give an answer to those who sent us? What do you say about yourself?" [23]He said, "I am a voice of one crying in the wilderness, 'make straight the way of the Lord,' as Isaiah the prophet said." [24]Now they had been sent from the Pharisees. [25]They asked him, and said to him, "Why then are you baptizing, if you are not the Christ, nor Elijah, nor the Prophet?" [26]John answered them saying, "I baptize in water, but among you stands One whom you do not know. [27]"It is He who comes after me, the thong of whose sandal I am not worthy to untie."

And so John the Baptist is the preparatory messenger spoken of in this passage. He prepared the way for the Lord's first coming which effectively dealt with the provision of salvation for all who would repent of their sins and trust in the Lord to rescue them from sin's curse and condemnation.

But this successful mission, topped off by the resurrection and ascension of Christ, prepared the way for His Second Coming-- which will be for the purpose of judgment.

Malachi's third point centers on this coming of the Lord in judgment in Malachi 3:1-5. Let's start with Malachi 3:1.

> *"Behold, I am going to send My messenger, and he will clear the way before Me. And the Lord, whom you seek, will suddenly come to His temple; and the messenger of the covenant, in whom you delight, behold, He is coming," says the Lord of hosts.*

There is a shift here from Christ's first coming to this earth as the suffering Messiah, coming to bear the sins of the world, preceded by the preparatory messenger of God, to His Second-Coming as the victorious Messiah who has come to reign over the earth and who has come in judgment.

At his first coming, He provided a sacrifice for the sins of the world. At His Second Coming, He will come in judgment of the world for its sins. He will come to purify and to judge.

Dr. Norman Geisler, a Christian apologist and philosopher who serves as the president of Southern Evangelical Seminary, says that there are 1,845 references to Christ's second coming in the Old Testament, where 17 books give it prominence. In the 260 chapters of the New Testament, there are 318 references to the second advent of Christ—an amazing 1 out of every 30 verses. Twenty-three of the 27 New Testament books refer to this great event. According to Galaxie Software's 10,000 Sermon

THE DANGER OF BEING DISAPPOINTED WITH GOD

Illustrations program, "For every prophecy in the Bible concerning Christ's first advent, there are eight which look forward to His second!"

Malachi describes this event as something that will happen suddenly. In the original language, the idea here is instantaneously and without expectation. The adverb is almost universally associated with an event that brings terrible loss, lasting distress or severe affliction. In other words, a disaster.

And then Malachi with a tone of sarcasm says *"the Lord you are seeking will come to his temple."* But the people of Malachi's day only sought the Messiah because of the prosperity that was associated with His coming.

The Temple referred to here is not the Temple of their time nor is it the Temple of Herod that existed during the life of Christ which was destroyed in AD 70. This is referring to <u>His</u> Temple, the Millennial Temple.

The Lord is also described as *the messenger of the covenant,* most likely a reference to the pre-incarnate appearance of our Lord to Abraham in which He promised to him a land, a people and a seed.

Let's continue to Malachi 3:2.

> *But who can endure the day of His coming? And who can stand when He appears? For He is like a refiner's fire and like fullers' soap.*

The day of His coming is the "Day of the Lord" which is mentioned so frequently in the Scriptures and is always associated with a time for divine judgment and punishment.

THE ORACLE OF MALACHI

Malachi will soon say in Malachi 4:5 that this day would be a "great and dreadful day."

Malachi asks who can endure the day of His coming. When I went through the book of Revelation, I was shocked at what this world will experience just prior to the second coming of Christ. Our world will pass through a time of unprecedented, catastrophic, universal destruction and then Jesus will come. Malachi asks, who can endure the day of his coming--after such an unleashing of God's righteous wrath on this world, who will be able to endure it?

Secondly, Malachi asks, "who can stand when He appears?"

Certainly the wicked people on planet earth will not be able to stand in the presence of a holy God--with His penetrating gaze into the wickedness of their hearts.

The cleansing work of the Lord that will take place in that day is depicted here in two ways--fire and soap.

The refiner's fire will burn off the slag of their iniquity and remove their impurities, and the soap will wash away the moral stains of their sins.

Malachi 3:3 tells us the Lord will begin his purifying process with the Levities, the priestly tribe of Israel.

> *He will sit as a smelter and purifier of silver, and He will purify the sons of Levi and refine them like gold and silver, so that they may present to the Lord offerings in righteousness.*

THE DANGER OF BEING DISAPPOINTED WITH GOD

In Malachi's day they are the ones who are leading the people astray--and into sin and moral defilement. At the time of the Second Coming of the Lord, they will be purified and refined as gold and silver. And their refining will spread to the whole nation.

According to this image, God will be like a refiner of silver. Workers of silver can still be seen today in oriental bazaars. They melt the ore in small portable furnaces. As the ore melts, the dross or the impurities rise to the top and is then scraped off by the refiner.

The workman keeps peering into the crucible, removing dross until he can see his face in the molten metal as in a mirror. Then he knows his work is done. God will apply the heat of affliction and discipline until He can see His image in His people.

The end result of the refining process, according to Malachi 3:4, is that the sacrifices offered in worship to the Lord will be righteous sacrifices.

> *Then the offering of Judah and Jerusalem will be pleasing to the Lord as in the days of old and as in former years.*

Unlike the sacrifices presented by the priests in Malachi's day, they will be acceptable.

The Jews of Malachi's day ask where the justice of God is. Verse 5 is their answer.

> *"Then I will draw near to you for judgment; and I will be a swift witness against the sorcerers and against the adulterers and against those who swear falsely, and*

against those who oppress the wage earner in his wages, the widow and the orphan, and those who turn aside the alien and do not fear Me," says the Lord of hosts.

They think that when the Messiah comes, He will judge the nations. But instead, the Lord will come in judgment of Israel first in order to provide a believing remnant ready to enter into the Millennium and to worship the Lord.

The indictment of moral perversion will be the quick work of the Lord. He will swiftly come as a witness against those who are sorcerers--that is, those who practice witchcraft and other forms of occult behavior in Israel--and those who commit adultery, which is a clear violation of the seventh commandment.

Perjury, or lying under oath and therefore corrupting justice, violated God's ninth commandment given in Exodus 20:16. God would come as a witness against those who lie under oath.

You shall not bear false witness against your neighbor.

Cheating the laborer out of his daily wages was a serious infraction of God's standard of morality as seen in Leviticus 19:13.

You shall not oppress your neighbor, nor rob him. The wages of a hired man are not to remain with you all night until morning.

And Deuteronomy 24:14-15.

[14]You shall not oppress a hired servant who is poor and needy, whether he is one of your countrymen or one of

*your aliens who is in your land in your towns. [15]You
shall give him his wages on his day before the sun sets,
for he is poor and sets his heart on it; so that he will not
cry against you to the Lord and it become sin in you.*

God takes it very personally when the poor, widows, orphans
and aliens are taken advantage of by the vultures of society and
justice is withheld from them.

All such moral perversion is a testimony of the fact that such
people do not fear God. Their behavior stands as a witness to
the fact that they do not have a profound reverence for God that
prompts obedience and submission to His standards. They do
not have a fear of living beyond His will.

Such people will be shocked, stunned, stupefied and frightened
out of their wits when the Lord comes a second time for
judgment.

Malachi's fourth and final point in this section, found in
Malachi 3:6, centers on the character of a changeless God.

*For I, the Lord do not change; therefore you, O sons of
Jacob, are not consumed.*

God is making one thing very clear here. The longevity of the
history of Israel is not because of the people of Israel but rather
because of their relationship with a covenant-keeping God
whose character remains unchanged and whose promises are
forever sure.

It's for this reason that a people like Israel have not exhausted
the patience of God to the point of their own destruction.

THE ORACLE OF MALACHI

When the Scriptures declare that God is unchangeable it means that He is perpetually the same in the perfection of His character. God does not evolve or improve because perfection of nature is not subject to such a process.

God will never become wiser, more holy, more just, more merciful, more loving or more truthful.

God is unchangeable in His character, His word, His purposes and His promises.

Balaam, in Numbers 23:19, under divine inspiration declared truth.

> *God is not a man, that He should lie, nor a son of man, that He should change His mind. Does He speak and then not act? Does He promise and not fulfill? (NIV)*

Again, Samuel the prophet and priest declared to King Saul, as recorded in 1 Samuel 15:29.

> *He who is the Glory of Israel does not lie or change His mind; for He is not a man, that He should change His mind. (NIV)*

James speaks of the unchangeable character of God in James 1:17.

> **God is unchangeable in His character, His word, His purposes and His promises.**

> *Every good and perfect gift is from above, coming down from the Father of the heavenly lights, who does not change like shifting shadows. (NIV)*

The Psalmist said of the Lord in Psalm 102:25-27.

THE DANGER OF BEING DISAPPOINTED WITH GOD

> *25 In the beginning you laid the foundations of the earth, and the heavens are the work of your hands. 26 They will perish, but you remain; they will all wear out like a garment. Like clothing you will change them and they will be discarded. 27 But you remain the same, and your years will never end. (NIV)*

Israel owed its long history to this attribute of God. As obstinate and stubborn and disobedient as they were from time to time, they could not force change in an unchangeable God. He kept His covenant promises even when they did not keep their love, loyalty and obedience to Him.

So what does this mean for us?

First, we are not to assume that the delay of God's just judgment means that unjust sinners have escaped the day of reckoning before the tribunal of God because they are presently prosperous.

Second, we are most susceptible to distorting the character of God in our minds when we allow the circumstances of life to formulate our theology.

And third, the best way to be properly prepared for Christ Second Coming--which will be a time of judgment--is by responding biblically to His First Coming, which effectively achieved salvation from the condemnation to come.

THE ORACLE OF MALACHI

Chapter 7
The Sermon on the Amount

A minister tells the story of a preacher who asked a man why he did not join the church. The reply was that the thief dying on the cross next to Jesus did not join the church and he was saved.

"Well," said the minister, "if you do not belong to a church, perhaps you can help by supporting missions?" "No," said the man. "The dying thief did not help missions, and wasn't he saved?"

"Yes," said the minister, "I suppose he was, but you must remember that he was a dying thief, whereas you are a living one."

In Malachi 3:7-12, the Lord indicts the Jews of Malachi's day of robbing Him. Their unwillingness to obey God in this important area was just another manifestation that they were in desperate need of spiritual revival and renewal.

> [7] *"From the days of your fathers you have turned aside from My statutes and have not kept them. Return to Me, and I will return to you," says the Lord of hosts. "But you say, 'How shall we return?'* [8] *Will a man rob God? Yet you are robbing Me! But you say, 'How have we robbed You?' In tithes and offerings.* [9] *You are cursed with a curse, for you are robbing Me, the whole nation of you!* [10] *Bring the whole tithe into the storehouse, so that there may be food in My house, and test Me now in this," says the Lord of hosts, "if I will not open for you the windows of heaven and pour out for you a blessing*

until it overflows. ¹¹ Then I will rebuke the devourer for you, so that it will not destroy the fruits of the ground; nor will your vine in the field cast its grapes," says the Lord of hosts. ¹² "All the nations will call you blessed, for you shall be a delightful land," says the Lord of hosts.

A middle aged husband and wife are driving down the road. When they pull up to the stop light they can't help notice the young couple in the car next to them, sitting next to one another, his arm around her, and they were kissing while waiting for the light to turn green. The wife looks over at her husband who is driving and says "You remember when we used to do that?" And the husband says, "Yea, I remember."
And the wife says "how come we don't do that anymore?" The husband replies, "I'm not the one who moved."

This same sort of thing can happen with our relationship with the Lord. I am sure that a frequently repeated conversation with the Lord in prayer goes something like this.

"Lord, I remember when I couldn't get enough of Your Word and when I couldn't keep from telling everybody how You saved me and their need to be saved; when I could sense that I was growing closer and closer to You every day as I consumed Your Word and obeyed Your Word. Lord, what happened to my spiritual fervency? How come it's not that way today?"

And the Lord would be justified in saying "I'm not the one who moved!"

One area of our lives that can indicate there is a serious need for spiritual renewal is how we handle the blessings God has bestowed upon us. In other words, your stewardship of your time, talent and treasure is often a reflection of your current spiritual condition.

You can tell much about the spiritual life of someone by just taking note of how they use money and other resources that God has graciously bestowed upon them.

The Jews of Malachi's day are so disappointed with their current condition after returning from 70 years of captivity, that they have become skeptical of God's promises and even God's character.

Their skepticism manifests itself in that they are careless in worship (1:7), indifferent to the truth (2:6-7), disobedient to the covenant (2:10), faithless in their marriages (2:15) and stingy in their offerings (3:8).

This situation prompts God to speak directly to them about their need for spiritual renewal and their need to trust the Lord to bless them beyond their imagination--if they would only obey Him in this matter of required tithes and offerings.

I've divided the Lord's message to them and to us into three points. And an important truth emerges from this text--and that is that our God is the God of second chances.

Therefore, no matter how far you have strayed from the Lord, there is always the ability to return to Him and to start anew.

God's Call for Repentance

Essentially what is being conveyed in Malachi 3:6-7 is that God is unchangeable in holiness and they are unchangeable in their disobedience.

> [6] *"For I, the Lord, do not change; therefore you, O sons of Jacob, are not consumed.* [7] *From the days of your fathers you have turned aside from My statutes and have not kept them. Return to Me, and I will return to you,"* *says the Lord of hosts. "But you say, 'How shall we return?'"*

Based upon their current unfavorable circumstances and conditions, they have imagined that God has turned away from them, when in fact the truth is that they have turned away from God. And they have a history of turning away from God that goes all the way back to the time of their forefathers– like Moses, Joshua and others.

God calls upon them to return to Him and then He will return to them--in spite of their long history of willful disobedience, in spite of their questioning of God's love, treating the altar of the Lord with contempt in flagrant disobedience to God's statues regarding the sacrifices that should be present to him, divorcing their wives of their youth in order to marry pagan women, and trying His patience to the point of exhaustion by calling to question the very justice of God.

He still appeals to them to return to Him--which speaks of the incredible patience of God and His mercy and grace.

Returning to God in repentance is the first step in reconciling your relationship with the Lord. One needs to undergo a U-turn in his or her thinking about sin, self and the mandates of God.

This is the formula to a fresh start.

How did the Jews of Malachi's day respond to God's call for repentance? They declare obstinately, *"How shall we return?"*

The implication being that they have never left the Lord. Why do they need to return to Him? From their perspective He has left them.

This mindset is the death-knell of any hope of spiritual renewal.

God has no other recourse than to point to one glaring example of Israel's need to turn to the Lord in repentance and obedience. He addresses Israel's failure to obey God in reference to the tithes and offerings that lawfully belong to Him by divine mandate.

God's Charge of Robbery

Let's look again at Malachi 3:8-9.

> *[8] Will a man rob God? Yet you are robbing Me! But you say, "How have we robbed You?" In tithes and offerings. [9] You are cursed with a curse, for you are robbing Me, the whole nation of you!*

Essentially, God's charge against Israel is that they are thieves. It's bad enough to take unlawfully what belongs to someone else--but they are stealing from God!

The word "rob" in the original language means to take secretly and without permission the property of someone else--to steal what rightfully belongs to someone else. In this case it is to steal from God Himself.

And when confronted with the charge, from an omniscient God, they once again respond to His indictment in an indignant manner.

THE ORACLE OF MALACHI

"How do we rob you?"

The Lord responds by stating they rob Him of the required tithes and offerings.

According to instructions given to Israel by God earlier in the Old Testament, there were several mandated tithes and offerings that the nation was to give in order to sustain the theocracy and to support the Levitical priesthood, the various national festivals and to meet the needs of the poor.

Obviously, a self-sufficient God has no need of these things for Himself. But in His profound wisdom, He set up the system of tithes and offerings in order to provide for the needs of others.

The word "tithe" refers to a tenth part of the whole. And in the case of the nation of Israel living in an agrarian culture, this amounts to a tenth of their livestock and a tenth of their produce.

You can find the specific instructions in Leviticus 27:30.

> *A tithe of everything from the land, whether grain from the soil or fruit from the trees, belongs to the Lord; it is holy to the Lord. (NIV)*

And Leviticus 27:32.

> *The entire tithe of the herd and flock—every tenth animal that passes under the shepherd's rod—will be holy to the Lord. (NIV)*

This was not free-will giving but required giving. It is sort of like a national tax as the nation functioned under the rule of the Lord.

From the tithes and offerings, the Levites, priests, orphans, widows, and aliens were supported as recorded in Deuteronomy 14:27-29.

> *[27] And do not neglect the Levites living in your towns, for they have no allotment or inheritance of their own. [28] At the end of every three years, bring all the tithes of that year's produce and store it in your towns, [29] so that the Levites (who have no allotment or inheritance of their own) and the aliens, the fatherless and the widows who live in your towns may come and eat and be satisfied, and so that the Lord your God may bless you in all the work of your hands. (NIV)*

From the tithe given to the Levites, a tithe of that tithe was to be given to the priest in the Temple as seen in Numbers 18:25-29.

> *[25] The Lord said to Moses, [26] "Speak to the Levites and say to them: 'When you receive from the Israelites the tithe I give you as your inheritance, you must present a tenth of that tithe as the Lord's offering. [27] Your offering will be reckoned to you as grain from the threshing floor or juice from the winepress. [28] In this way you also will present an offering to the Lord from all the tithes you receive from the Israelites. From these tithes you must give the Lord's portion to Aaron the priest. [29] You must present as the Lord's portion the best and holiest part of everything given to you.'" (NIV)*

THE ORACLE OF MALACHI

The "offerings" were the portions of sacrifices which the priests were permitted to use for food as we can read in Exodus 29:27-28.

> [27] *Consecrate those parts of the ordination ram that belong to Aaron and his sons: the breast that was waved and the thigh that was presented.* [28] *This is always to be the regular share from the Israelites for Aaron and his sons. It is the contribution the Israelites are to make to the Lord from their fellowship offerings. (NIV)*

The Jews of Malachi's day have undoubtedly made some small contributions to the Levities and the temple service as a part of their ritualistic practice of religion. But according to Malachi 3:10, they have not given the whole tithe.

> *"Bring the whole tithe into the storehouse, so that there may be food in My house, and test Me now in this," says the Lord of hosts, "if I will not open for you the windows of heaven and pour out for you a blessing until it overflows.*

Thus they are robbing God of the tithes and offerings mandated in the Law and perhaps forcing the Levities to farm their land instead of devoting themselves to the ministry of the care for the Temple. Since the Levites are not getting the entire portion of tithe, the priests--who were the descendants of Aaron--are not getting the full tenth of tithe from the Levites.

And the poor, the widows, orphans and aliens in the land are essential left with little or no support at all.

THE DANGER OF BEING DISAPPOINTED WITH GOD

You can see the far reaching impact of what is happening when just one person chooses to live independent of God's will in such matters and this becomes a corporate characteristic.

This proves to us once again that when we sin we don't experience the consequences of our sin alone.

I can almost hear them say, "But times are bad, we were expecting prosperity when we returned to the Promised Land and instead we are experiencing tough economic times--certainly we are to be excused from giving the full amount of the tithes and offerings."

As a matter of fact, according to verse 9, their disobedience in this area is why they are experiencing such tough times.

> *You are cursed with a curse, for you are robbing Me, the whole nation of you!*

The whole nation is under a divine curse because they are robbing God. You get a sense of the nature of the curse from verse 11.

> *"Then I will rebuke the devourer for you, so that it will not destroy the fruits of the ground; nor will your vine in the field cast its grapes," says the Lord of hosts.*

Pests were devouring their crops and their vines were not producing any grapes. In an agrarian culture, this would be devastating.

But this should not have been a surprise to them. God had warned Israel, in Deuteronomy 28:38-40, that this would be the end result of their disobedience.

> *38 You will sow much seed in the field but you will harvest little, because locusts will devour it. 39 You will plant vineyards and cultivate them but you will not drink the wine or gather the grapes, because worms will eat them. 40 You will have olive trees throughout your country but you will not use the oil, because the olives will drop off. (NIV)*

By robbing God in this manner, they in the end are robbing themselves of the blessings of God.

But can we who make up the church rob God of tithes and offerings?

First, we must understand that mandated tithes and offerings was an Old Testament regulation for the nation of Israel as they functioned under a theocracy.

These regulations were not carried over into the New Testament to be observed by those who make up the church. There is no New Testament command mandating the church to give a tithe or several tithes such as required of Israel.

The church does not have a Levitical priesthood to support, nor do we have a high priest or a temple in need of our support. Nor do we have certain national religious festivals that we need to observe and support such as the nation of Israel had to do.

> **Our giving is to be regulated by our transformed hearts that are given to us as a part of the New Covenant. Our giving should be a product of being born again.**

THE DANGER OF BEING DISAPPOINTED WITH GOD

However, 1 Timothy 5:17-18 does give us some important guidance. We are required to support those who give themselves full time to the preaching and teaching of the Word.

> [17] *The elders who rule well are to be considered worthy of double honor, especially those who work hard at preaching and teaching.* [18] *For the Scripture says, "You shall not muzzle the ox while he is threshing," and "The laborer is worthy of his wages."*

We should also support the gospel ministry as we read very clearly in 1 Corinthians 9:13-14.

> [13] *Do you not know that those who perform sacred services eat the food of the temple, and those who attend regularly to the altar have their share from the altar?* [14] *So also the Lord directed those who proclaim the gospel to get their living from the gospel.*

We will always have the poor and as believers we demonstrate the love and mercy of Christ when we respond appropriately to the needs of the poor as shown in Ephesians 4:28.

> *He who steals must steal no longer; but rather he must labor, performing with his own hands what is good, so that he will have something to share with one who has need.*

But our giving is to be regulated by our transformed hearts that are given to us as a part of the New Covenant. Our giving should be a product of being born again.

We can rob God of what is properly His if our giving is not in accord with the principles of New Testament giving.

THE ORACLE OF MALACHI

First, our giving should be reflective of the complete surrender of ourselves to the Lord as reflected in 2 Corinthians 8:1-5.

> *[1] Now, brethren, we wish to make known to you the grace of God which has been given in the churches of Macedonia, [2] that in a great ordeal of affliction their abundance of joy and their deep poverty overflowed in the wealth of their liberality. [3] For I testify that according to their ability, and beyond their ability, they gave of their own accord, [4] begging us with much urging for the favor of participation in the support of the saints, [5] and this, not as we had expected, but they first gave themselves to the Lord and to us by the will of God.*

And in Romans 12:1.

> *Therefore I urge you, brethren, by the mercies of God, to present your bodies a living and holy sacrifice, acceptable to God, which is your spiritual service of worship.*

Second, our giving should be sacrificial. That is, it should cost us something and not be just giving out of our surplus. We can see these instructions in 2 Corinthians 8:3-4.

> *[3] For I testify that according to their ability, and beyond their ability, they gave of their own accord, [4] begging us with much urging for the favor of participation in the support of the saints.*

THE DANGER OF BEING DISAPPOINTED WITH GOD

And 2 Corinthians 8:9.

> *For you know the grace of our Lord Jesus Christ, that*
> *though He was rich, yet for your sake He became poor,*
> *so that you through His poverty might become rich.*

Third, according to 1 Corinthians 16:1-2, our giving should be in proportion to the blessings that God has bestowed upon us.

> *[1] Now concerning the collection for the saints, as I*
> *directed the churches of Galatia, so do you also. [2] On*
> *the first day of every week each one of you is to put*
> *aside and save, as he may prosper, so that no collections*
> *be made when I come.*

For many of us, that would mean that our giving would far exceed a tenth of our income.

Fourth, our giving should be an appropriate response to needs-- rather than a response to regulations as seen in 2 Corinthians 8:3-5.

> *[3] For I testify that according to their ability, and beyond*
> *their ability, they gave of their own accord, [4] begging us*
> *with much urging for the favor of participation in the*
> *support of the saints, [5] and this, not as we had expected,*
> *but they first gave themselves to the Lord and to us by*
> *the will of God.*

And Acts 4:34-35.

> *[34] For there was not a needy person among them, for all*
> *who were owners of land or houses would sell them and*
> *bring the proceeds of the sales [35] and lay them at the*

apostles' feet, and they would be distributed to each as any had need.

And 1 John 3:16-18.

[16] We know love by this, that He laid down His life for us; and we ought to lay down our lives for the brethren. [17] But whoever has the world's goods, and sees his brother in need and closes his heart against him, how does the love of God abide in him? [18] Little children, let us not love with word or with tongue, but in deed and truth.

As you can see, in the early church they responded to the needs of the poor not because of some regulation but because of regeneration and the transformation that took place in their hearts.

Fifth, our giving should be cheerful, faith based and grace empowered.

Some solid guidance in this area is found in 2 Corinthians 9:7-14.

[7] Each one must do just as he has purposed in his heart, not grudgingly or under compulsion, for God loves a cheerful giver. [8] And God is able to make all grace abound to you, so that always having all sufficiency in everything, you may have an abundance for every good deed; [9] as it is written, "He scattered abroad, He gave to the poor, His righteousness endures forever." [10] Now He who supplies seed to the sower and bread for food will supply and multiply your seed for sowing and increase the harvest of your righteousness; [11] you will be

enriched in everything for all liberality, which through us is producing thanksgiving to God. [12] *For the ministry of this service is not only fully supplying the needs of the saints, but is also overflowing through many thanksgivings to God.* [13] *Because of the proof given by this ministry, they will glorify God for your obedience to your confession of the gospel of Christ and for the liberality of your contribution to them and to all,* [14] *while they also, by prayer on your behalf, yearn for you because of the surpassing grace of God in you.*

I am convinced by Scripture that if our giving is not reflective of these principles, then we can rob ourselves of the blessings that God bestows upon those who give in this way.

God's Challenge for Renewal

Now we move to Malachi 3:10-12.

[10] *"Bring the whole tithe into the storehouse, so that there may be food in My house, and test Me now in this," says the Lord of hosts, "if I will not open for you the windows of heaven and pour out for you a blessing until it overflows.* [11] *Then I will rebuke the devourer for you, so that it will not destroy the fruits of the ground; nor will your vine in the field cast its grapes," says the Lord of hosts.* [12] *"All the nations will call you blessed, for you shall be a delightful land," says the Lord of hosts.*

THE ORACLE OF MALACHI

This particular section reminds me of the old hymn that exhorts us to trust and obey, for there's no other way, to be happy in Jesus, but to trust and obey.

The Lord is mandating them to bring the whole tithe into the storehouse. All the tithe. In other words, a partial compliance is insufficient! Obey God entirely in this matter. Give what He has commanded you to give.

In full compliance, they are to bring the whole tithe into the storehouse which was an actual place in the Temple were the produce and livestock were placed and made available to the Levites, the priests and the poor. This was the Temple treasury.

If they will obey God in this area there would be food available in God's house. The Levites, the priests and the poor will have all that they need in order to sustain life.

> In the church today, there is no requirement for a tithe, and you are not under a curse if you don't tithe to a church.
>
> Today, under grace, our giving is governed by our new nature in Christ. We should give because we want to, and if we don't it directly reflects our spiritual condition.
>
> We give because we love God. We give because we are driven to by our love for God and our love for others.

And the nation of Israel will have more than what they need, as promised in verses 10-11.

THE DANGER OF BEING DISAPPOINTED WITH GOD

The word *test* is a translation of the Hebrew word *bachan* which means to examine, scrutinize, to test, prove, try. It would be equivalent to saying, "Try me in this and I will prove to be faithful."

If they will test God in this area by giving the whole tithes and offerings, God promises to bless them in such a way that the nations will notice and declare them to be a blessed and prosperous land.

According to Walvoord and Zuck in their Bible Knowledge Commentary, "These blessings would include agricultural prosperity—good crops not destroyed by pests, and undamaged vines (Mal. 3:11) —and a good reputation among all the nations (Mal. 3:12). These blessings simply awaited their obedience."

But the bottom line is that they must obey God in this required giving and trust God in spite of the current economic situation. They need to be willing to try God in this matter.

This then would be the actions of returning to God and the beginning of spiritual renewal.

So, before we move on through Malachi, we should pause and contemplate the truths that God has shown us in His Word.

First, your giving is an expression of your current spiritual condition. Not obeying God in this area clearly indicates that you are in need of a new level of intimacy with the Lord.

Second, giving sacrificially and in proportion to the blessings you receive from the gracious hand of God is the response of a regenerated heart--not regulations or requirements.

THE ORACLE OF MALACHI

Third, in robbing God, you rob yourself of His blessings.

And fourth, the amount of your giving must be an expression of your trust in the Lord rather than a reaction to your current financial situation.

Chapter 8
God Hears You!

This story is told of President Franklin Roosevelt, who often endured long receiving lines at the White House. He complained that no one really paid any attention to what was said. One day, during a reception, he decided to try an experiment. To each person who came down the line and shook his hand, he murmured, "I murdered my grandmother this morning." The guests responded with phrases like, "Marvelous!", "Keep up the good work.", "We are proud of you." and "God bless you, sir."

It was not till the end of the line, while greeting the ambassador from Bolivia, that his words were actually heard. Perplexed, the ambassador leaned over and whispered, "I'm sure she had it coming Mr. President."

Listening, really listening to others can be a challenge in our world of communication overload and with our preoccupied minds submerged by the worries and cares of the day. But listening, really listening is never a problem with God.

Because our God is omniscient, He knows all things perfectly, simultaneously, independently and innately. And because our God is omnipresent, He hears all things perfectly because all that is said is said in His presence.

He is the ancient of days but His hearing never grows dim. Those who have right standing with God find comfort in that truth.

THE ORACLE OF MALACHI

Psalm 34:17 tells us a profound truth.

> *The righteous cry out, and the Lord hears them; He delivers them from all their troubles. (NIV)*

Proverbs 15:29 also confirms the same truth.

> *The Lord is far from the wicked but He hears the prayer of the righteous. (NIV)*

I guess I've always been conscious of the fact that God hears my prayers. But I'm not always aware that God also hears my everyday conversation. God hears when I am grumbling about Him in regards to my current lot in life.

We see this clearly in Exodus 16:1-9, where God has Moses tell the people of Israel over and over that He has heard their grumblings.

> *¹ Then they set out from Elim, and all the congregation of the sons of Israel came to the wilderness of Sin, which is between Elim and Sinai, on the fifteenth day of the second month after their departure from the land of Egypt. ² The whole congregation of the sons of Israel grumbled against Moses and Aaron in the wilderness. ³ The sons of Israel said to them, "Would that we had died by the Lord's hand in the land of Egypt, when we sat by the pots of meat, when we ate bread to the full; for you have brought us out into this wilderness to kill this whole assembly with hunger." ⁴ Then the Lord said to Moses, "Behold, I will rain bread from heaven for you; and the people shall go out and gather a day's portion every day, that I may test them, whether or not they will walk in My instruction. ⁵ On the sixth day, when they*

prepare what they bring in, it will be twice as much as they gather daily." [6] So Moses and Aaron said to all the sons of Israel, "At evening you will know that the Lord has brought you out of the land of Egypt; [7] and in the morning you will see the glory of the Lord, for He hears your grumblings against the Lord; and what are we, that you grumble against us?" [8] Moses said, "This will happen when the Lord gives you meat to eat in the evening, and bread to the full in the morning; for the Lord hears your grumblings which you grumble against Him. And what are we? Your grumblings are not against us but against the Lord." [9] Then Moses said to Aaron, "Say to all the congregation of the sons of Israel, 'Come near before the Lord, for He has heard your grumblings.'"

Malachi 3:13-18 indicates that it's impossible to gossip about God without God hearing your gossip.

[13] *"Your words have been arrogant against Me," says the Lord. "Yet you say, 'What have we spoken against You?' [14] You have said, 'It is vain to serve God; and what profit is it that we have kept His charge, and that we have walked in mourning before the Lord of hosts? [15] So now we call the arrogant blessed; not only are the doers of wickedness built up but they also test God and escape.'" [16] Then those who feared the Lord spoke to one another, and the Lord gave attention and heard it, and a book of remembrance was written before Him for those who fear the Lord and who esteem His name. [17] "They will be Mine," says the Lord of hosts, "on the day that I prepare My own possession, and I will spare them as a man spares his own son who serves him." [18] So you will again distinguish between the righteous and the wicked,*

THE ORACLE OF MALACHI

> *between one who serves God and one who does not
> serve Him.*

God was eavesdropping on the Nation of Israel during the days
of Malachi and He heard the conversation between those who
had turned their backs on Him--disappointed because of their
current situation. He also heard those who remained faithful
servants of the Lord no matter what the majority view of God in
Israel was at that time and no matter their current
circumstances.

I know that when it comes to testing the genuineness of one's
saving relationship with God, we frequently point to the
conduct of one's life as a means to verify the reality of such
union. But did you know that your conversation, especially
about God and His purposes, is also revealing of your true
spiritual condition?

One's conversation about God and the outworking of His
providence serves as an indicator of the current condition of
your relationship with Him, and your level of trust in Him.

In Malachi 3:13-18, we will see two ways in which
conversations about God manifest the true spiritual condition of
those who profess to know God.

What you say about God is important because it is a reflection
of what you think about God. And what you think about God is
the most important thing you can think.

Our conversation about God can reveal our true motive for
serving Him. Read Malachi 3:13-15 again, this time in the NIV
translation.

THE DANGER OF BEING DISAPPOINTED WITH GOD

> [13] *"You have said harsh things against me," says the Lord. "Yet you ask, 'What have we said against you?' [14] You have said, 'It is futile to serve God. What did we gain by carrying out his requirements and going about like mourners before the Lord Almighty? [15] But now we call the arrogant blessed. Certainly the evildoers prosper, and even those who challenge God escape.'"* (NIV)

You will recall from the previous chapters that God indicts the Jews of Malachi's day of robbing Him of the required tithes and offerings. With his indictment, God issues a challenge to bring the whole tithe into the storehouse--or the Temple treasury--and test God in this area. God says they will see that He will open the floodgates of heaven and pour out so many blessings that they will not be able to find room for all of it if they will only obey Him and trust Him in this.

Unfortunately, the majority of the Jews of that day have grown so disappointed with their current situation and so skeptical of God and His promises, that they are in no mood to respond to God's challenge.

Their skepticism has flourished into irreverent cynicism, especially as it pertains to the value of serving the Lord. And this is reflected in their comments made about the Lord and serving Him.

In Malachi 3:13, God omnisciently says to them, "You have said harsh things against

> **What you say about God is important because it is a reflection of what you think about God. And what you think about God is the most important thing you can think.**

me." The NASB translates this verse, "your words have been arrogant against me." Harsh and arrogant are a translation of a Hebrew word that coveys the idea of being strong--they are words that are overbearing, over-the-top and overstated.

Such conversations would fall into the category of being blasphemous and disrespectful.

We use this expression in our day when someone makes a harsh comment about someone or something and we respond by saying, "Those are strong words."

And, as has been their pattern throughout the book of Malachi, the Jews of Malachi's day respond in a defensive manner in Malachi 3:13b.

> *What have we said against you?*

And so, in Malachi 3:14, the Lord restates the conversations that these people have with each other that He hears while in the glory of His heavenly abode.

> *You have said, "It is futile to serve God. What did we gain by carrying out his requirements and going about like mourners before the Lord Almighty?" (NIV)*

The skeptics' contention--manifested in their conversations with each other--is that it does not pay to render service to the Lord. As a matter of fact, it is futile or vain, which is a translation of the Hebrew word *Shav*--which refers to that which is empty and without a profitable outcome that is justly reflective of your efforts.

No wonder their sacrifices are subpar and their worship is so mechanical. They view serving the Lord as being useless, valueless, and materially and spiritually worthless.

In other words, their service rendered to God is done in anticipation of some sort of payment from God. It is not rendered out of love, or out of worship, or out of a pursuit of His glory or in anticipation of future eternal rewards.

The true motive for serving and worshipping the Lord is what they can get from the Lord. They anticipate that God owes them for their compliance to His requirements. They believe they are entitled to a carefree and abundantly blessed life and God is not living up to His end of the bargain.

The people expect their religiosity to pay big dividends.

They expect material and spiritual prosperity in spite of the fact that they are careless and contemptuous in their worship, indifferent to God and His Word, disobedient to the covenant, faithless in their marriages, stingy in their tithes and offerings, and under the curse of God for such things.

They prove Satan's point made in the book of Job that some people serve God only for what they might get from God. If you take away their blessings, they will turn on God in a heartbeat.

These skeptics further allege that carrying out God's requirements as it pertains to their service in the temple and their sacrifices have resulted in no real profit, no increase, and no observable return in material prosperity or political influence.

They are still under the rule of the Persians and not the Messiah. They are experiencing poverty, drought and economic adversity and not prosperity. So why abide by God's requirements if this is the outcome?

They further allege that going about like mourners before the Lord yields no benefits either. They no longer see any value in mourning over their sins, either personally or nationally like those who had returned from captivity did--100 years earlier.

In other words, what's the value of repentance from your sins if there is no immediate reward of divine blessing? The implication is that God owes you something because you have recognized your sinfulness and have mourned over your sin.

Their claimed proof of the futility in serving the Lord is the life situations of the arrogant and the evildoers in comparison with theirs. Once again, we see the danger of framing your perspective of God and His provisions and promises through the grid of your current circumstances and your interpretation of them, as recorded in Malachi 3:15.

> *But now we call the arrogant blessed. Certainly the evildoers prosper, and even those who challenge God escape. (NIV)*

God declares that He will bless them so abundantly that they can not contain all that He will bestow on them if they will obey Him by bringing the whole tithe into the storehouse. Even the surrounding nations will have to acknowledge that the hand of God's blessings is upon them.

But the skeptics now mockingly pronounce that the arrogant are blessed and the evildoers are the truly prosperous and that those who challenge God with blatant disregard of His commands go unpunished--that they escape God's judgment. God seems impotent to do anything about their disregard of His standards.

In other words, they're the ones who are blessed by God not us. So what's the advantage of serving the Lord?

This kind of thinking is akin to what they had stated previously in Malachi 2:17.

> *You have wearied the Lord with your words. Yet you say, "How have we wearied Him?" In that you say, "Everyone who does evil is good in the sight of the Lord, and He delights in them," or, "Where is the God of justice?"*

This is the kind of thinking about God and His provisions that is born out of measuring the temporal as of greater value than the eternal, and forgetting that those who know God have a far greater destiny than those who are lost and yet possess the many temporal treasures of this world.

For the majority of the Jews during the days of Malachi, serving Jehovah is evaluated on a dollars-and-cents basis. If they are not blessed with material prosperity, then one might as well not serve or worship the Lord.

In other words, if God is to be served and worshiped, it's going to cost Him something.

Let's keep moving forward, and continue to Malachi 3:16-18.

> *[16] Then those who feared the Lord spoke to one another, and the Lord gave attention and heard it, and a book of*

> *remembrance was written before Him for those who fear the Lord and who esteem His name.* [17] *"They will be Mine," says the Lord of hosts, "on the day that I prepare My own possession, and I will spare them as a man spares his own son who serves him."* [18] *So you will again distinguish between the righteous and the wicked, between one who serves God and one who does not serve Him.*

Just as God has heard the conversation of the arrogant mockers and cynics, He has also listened to the conversations of those who fear Him and honor His name.

Once again we see that God always has His faithful remnant. Even in the darkest days of Israel's spiritual condition, there are always those who love the Lord comprehensively and fear the Lord continuously.

But what does it mean to fear the Lord? The Hebrew word translated "fear" is yare. The word conveys the idea of simply being afraid, but it also projects the idea of reverence, or to stand in awe of God, or to honor and worship God.

From the many different ways that the fear of Lord is used in Scripture, this attitude can be rightly defined as a chosen mind set about God that incorporates reverence, awe, veneration, wonder, admiration and apprehension. It is a steady, consistent mind set which remains unaltered by one's feelings or circumstances at any given time.

> **To fear the Lord means to be afraid, in reverence, standing in awe, and honoring and worshipping God.**

THE DANGER OF BEING DISAPPOINTED WITH GOD

The fear of the Lord also incorporates a wholesome dread of living independent of God's will--knowing that God loves his children too much to allow them to continuously disobey His will. So the fear of the Lord is a mixture of reverential awe and fear.

To fear God is to respect Him enough to care what He says and be afraid enough to submit to His authority.

John Murray has rightly stated that, "The fear of God is the soul of godliness. That is, the fear of God is the animating and invigorating principles of a godly life. It is the wellspring of all godly desires and aspirations."

It proves to us once again that what you think about God is the most important thing you think.
The fear of the Lord and the possession of wisdom are inseparably linked in the Scriptures.

Proverbs 9:10 tells us about this fear.

> *The fear of the Lord is the beginning of wisdom, and knowledge of the Holy One is understanding. (NIV)*

Exodus 20:18-20 tells us this mindset toward God serves as a sin deterrent.

> [18] *When the people saw the thunder and lightning and heard the trumpet and saw the mountain in smoke, they trembled with fear. They stayed at a distance* [19] *and said to Moses, "Speak to us yourself and we will listen. But do not have God speak to us or we will die."* [20] *Moses said to the people, "Do not be afraid. God has come to*

test you, so that the fear of God will be with you to keep you from sinning." (NIV)

And so does Proverbs 16:6.

Through love and faithfulness sin is atoned for; through the fear of the Lord a man avoids evil. (NIV)

It is also the fear of the Lord that prompts us to hate what God hates.

Proverbs 8:13 tells us more about this.

To fear the Lord is to hate evil; I hate pride and arrogance, evil behavior and perverse speech. (NIV)

To fear the Lord increases the potential of living a long life, as written in Proverbs 10:27.

The fear of the Lord adds length to life, but the years of the wicked are cut short. (NIV)

And Proverbs 14:27.

The fear of the Lord is a fountain of life, turning a man from the snares of death. (NIV)

Proverbs 22:4 tells us it is this mindset coupled with humility that brings prosperity to our lives.

Humility and the fear of the Lord bring wealth and honor and life. (NIV)

THE DANGER OF BEING DISAPPOINTED WITH GOD

King Solomon, in Ecclesiastes 12:13 even declared that fearing the Lord and keeping His commandments is the whole duty of mankind.

> *The conclusion, when all has been heard, is: fear God and keep His commandments, because this applies to every person.*

But the skeptic and the cynics of Malachi's day did not heed the instructions given in Proverbs 23:17.

> *Do not let your heart envy sinners, But live in the fear of the Lord always.*

Those who fear the Lord are talking with each other but they are certainly not conscious of the fact that God is listening to their conversation. They are not praying to God but talking to each other about God.

We are not told of the content of their conversation but we are told of the mindset of those who are conversing. They fear the Lord and so no doubt their conversation reflects their reverence, honor, awe, respect and adoration of God--and their submission to His authority.

They honor His name. The word *honored* is a translation of the Hebrew word, *chashab* which basically means to think. In this context, it refers to a mind-set of value and high esteem. They think of God so as to regard Him with great esteem.

They give to God what He asks the priests of Malachi's day to give to Him--honor! And so names are taken. A registry of those who fear the Lord during these days when the majority are disappointed with God, doubting His promises and skeptical of

THE ORACLE OF MALACHI

His blessings. These people, as few as they are, maintain the proper mindset toward God in spite of the circumstances and in spite of what is going on around them.

A scroll of remembrance is made, in the presence of God, of those who fear Him and honor His name in order that they may be properly rewarded for their mindset in the future.

Perhaps this scroll is similar to the Persian custom of entering into a book all acts that should be rewarded in the future.

Let's look at Malachi 3:16-18 again.

> [16] *Then those who feared the Lord spoke to one another, and the Lord gave attention and heard it, and a book of remembrance was written before Him for those who fear the Lord and who esteem His name.* [17] *"They will be Mine," says the Lord of hosts, "on the day that I prepare My own possession, and I will spare them as a man spares his own son who serves him."* [18] *So you will again distinguish between the righteous and the wicked, between one who serves God and one who does not serve Him.*

In verse 17 we see that those who fear God and honor His name belong to the Lord and that will be clearly manifested on the day of the Lord. In that Day of Judgment, it will be clearly revealed that they are God's treasured possession. Treasured possession is a translation of one word from the Hebrew, *câgullah*, which refers to valued property or a peculiar treasure. And they will be spared from the judgment associated with the Day of The Lord at His second coming.

THE DANGER OF BEING DISAPPOINTED WITH GOD

And verse 18 tells us that on that day a clear distinction will be made between those who stand right with God and serve Him because they love and fear Him--and those who are wicked and perhaps attempted to serve the Lord with the wrong motives. The godly are characterized by their fear of the Lord; they honor the name of the Lord; they are liberated from the coming judgment of the Lord; they are righteous; and they willingly serve the Lord.

The ungodly are characterized by their harsh words against the Lord, a lack of value for serving the Lord or obeying His requirements, their envy of the wicked and they are the focus of God's judgment to come.

This section of Malachi clearly shows us that what you think and say about God provide a clear indication as to where you stand with Him.

It shows that God is far more interested in why you serve Him than how you serve Him.

It shows that your perspective of God must not be shaped by your read of your current circumstances and your perception of the "care-free" life of the wicked. Instead, you must view God on the basis of His self-revelation as it is given in His Word.

And finally, that those who stand right with God are those who fear the Lord, honor His name, serve Him with all their hearts and speak of Him with reverence and respect.

THE ORACLE OF MALACHI

Chapter 9
The Question of Destination

Let's begin this chapter by reading Malachi 4:1-6.

> [1] *"For behold, the day is coming, burning like a furnace;*
> *and all the arrogant and every evildoer will be chaff;*
> *and the day that is coming will set them ablaze," says*
> *the Lord of hosts, "so that it will leave them neither root*
> *nor branch.* [2] *But for you who fear My name, the sun of*
> *righteousness will rise with healing in its wings; and*
> *you will go forth and skip about like calves from the*
> *stall.* [3] *You will tread down the wicked, for they will be*
> *ashes under the soles of your feet on the day which I am*
> *preparing," says the Lord of hosts.* [4] *"Remember the law*
> *of Moses My servant, even the statutes and ordinances*
> *which I commanded him in Horeb for all Israel.* [5]
> *Behold, I am going to send you Elijah the prophet*
> *before the coming of the great and terrible day of the*
> *Lord.* [6] *He will restore the hearts of the fathers to their*
> *children and the hearts of the children to their fathers,*
> *so that I will not come and smite the land with a curse."*

In most of the manuscripts and editions of the Hebrew Bible, the whole of Malachi chapter 4 is treated as a continuation of chapter 3. That is to say, there is no chapter division as is common in our modern English translations.

> **God is far more interested in why you serve Him than how you serve Him.**

THE ORACLE OF MALACHI

In Malachi 3:18, God speaks of the distinction between the righteous and the wicked, between those who serve God and those who do not. In the fourth chapter, the Lord addresses the way and the time when such a distinction will be very clear.

So, as we approach the end of the book of Malachi, it is good to stop and think about the fact that this is the last message of the Old Testament prophets.

After this prophetic word, there would be 400 years of silence--in terms of new revelation from God--until the voice of John the Baptist is heard calling Israel to repentance in view of the coming of the Messiah.

The majority of the Jews during the days of Malachi have become estranged from God because of their dissatisfaction with their current situation. They think that by now, 100 years after returning from captivity, they should be faring far better than they are.

They are still under the rule of Persians and not the Messiah. The glory days of Israel are a fading memory. Instead of prosperity, they are encountering economic difficulty.

They have grown cynical and skeptical of God and His promises. And they consider the wicked and the evildoers as the ones who are truly blessed.

They even say that God favors such people.

And they can no longer see the advantage of serving the Lord.

THE DANGER OF BEING DISAPPOINTED WITH GOD

This mindset leads them to dishonor God, to disobey God and to no longer trust God. Instead of pursuing greater intimacy with the Lord, they distance themselves even more from Him.

In many ways, they are like some professing Christians of our day--who have grown weary because of their current difficult situation or who have experienced a great disappointment in this sin cursed earth. Or who have suffered a great loss--such as the death of a loved one--and their hurting hearts begin to entertain the same kind of thoughts.

How then can we break the pattern of this spiritually destructive way of thinking? What is the antidote to this venomous thought pattern of being envious of the wicked and critical of God?

According to the teaching of God's word, the best way to overcome this spiritually destructive thought pattern is to take note of these two contrasting destinies, to take thought of the eternal condition of the wicked in contrast to the eternal bliss of the righteous.

It is this truth that freed the psalmist Asaph from this oppressive and depressing way of thinking when he finds himself envying the wicked, as recorded in Psalm 73:16-19.

> [16] *When I pondered to understand this,*
> *it was troublesome in my sight*
> [17] *Until I came into the sanctuary of God;*
> *Then I perceived their end.*
> [18] *Surely You set them in slippery places;*
> *You cast them down to destruction*
> [19] *How they are destroyed in a moment!*
> *They are utterly swept away by sudden terrors!*

THE ORACLE OF MALACHI

Many of the Bible writers, while addressing people who are in the midst of some sort of tribulation, exhort them to be future minded as opposed to being overwhelmed by their read of their present circumstances, as in 1 Peter 1:3-6.

> *3 Blessed be the God and Father of our Lord Jesus Christ, who according to His great mercy has caused us to be born again to a living hope through the resurrection of Jesus Christ from the dead, 4 to obtain an inheritance which is imperishable and undefiled and will not fade away, reserved in heaven for you, 5 who are protected by the power of God through faith for a salvation ready to be revealed in the last time. 6 In this you greatly rejoice, even though now for a little while, if necessary, you have been distressed by various trials.*

And Romans 8:18.

> *For I consider that the sufferings of this present time are not worthy to be compared with the glory that is to be revealed to us.*

In other words, we should consider the eternal blessings of the righteous rather than the temporal blessings of the wicked. We must ask, what is the length of this life in comparison to eternity?

> **The biblical definition of hope is "confident expectation."**

This is the essence of the New Testament concept of hope.

I have divided Malachi 4:1-5 into four sections in order to capture the primary points being made here. And to highlight the truth that the best way to deal with being perplexed by the perceived blessed condition of the wicked is to take note of their destiny of eternal torment and the blissful destiny of the righteous.

Let's read the entire section again, and then we can dig into the verses.

> [1] *"For behold, the day is coming, burning like a furnace; and all the arrogant and every evildoer will be chaff; and the day that is coming will set them ablaze," says the Lord of hosts, "so that it will leave them neither root nor branch.* [2] *But for you who fear My name, the sun of righteousness will rise with healing in its wings; and you will go forth and skip about like calves from the stall.* [3] *You will tread down the wicked, for they will be ashes under the soles of your feet on the day which I am preparing," says the Lord of hosts.* [4] *"Remember the law of Moses My servant, even the statutes and ordinances which I commanded him in Horeb for all Israel.* [5] *Behold, I am going to send you Elijah the prophet before the coming of the great and terrible day of the Lord.*

The Heat of God's Judgment

For behold the day is coming.

Today might be a difficult day for you but behold the day is coming. You may be suffering and sorrowful today--but behold the day is coming. You may be perplexed and discouraged today--but behold the day is coming. You may be weary from your journey in this sin cursed world--but behold the day is coming. Injustice and moral decay may be all around you--but behold the day is coming.

THE ORACLE OF MALACHI

What day?

The great day of the Lord when the clear distinction will be made between those who fear the Lord and those who do not.

Read all of verse 1 again.

> *"For behold, the day is coming, burning like a furnace; and all the arrogant and every evildoer will be chaff; and the day that is coming will set them ablaze," says the Lord of hosts, "so that it will leave them neither root nor branch."*

This passage is speaking of that certain Day of Judgment in which those who are arrogant and wicked, or evildoers, will face the full and final outcome of their lost and sinful condition. This is frequently referred to as the Great Day of the Lord which I will speak more of later.

The point here is that no matter the present wealth, status, power or prestige of the arrogant and wicked, none of these temporal things will provide deliverance for them on that appointed day of God's wrath.

The Lord uses the imagery of a burning oven waiting to consume what is cast into it, only to quickly turn it into ashes. And the wicked and evildoers are described as chaff--which is the seed coverings and other debris separated from the seed in the process of threshing grain and is highly combustible.

Fire is a frequent symbol of judgment in the Scriptures. In Malachi 3:2, the Lord describes himself as a refiner's fire for the purpose of purification. But now we have the description of a furnace all ablaze for the purpose of condemnation and destruction.

The writer of the book of Hebrews warns those who have the privilege of receiving the knowledge of the truth (in particular, the truth of the Gospel message) have a day of terrifying judgment awaiting them in the future.

We read this in Hebrews 10:26-27.

> [26] *If we deliberately keep on sinning after we have received the knowledge of the truth, no sacrifice for sins is left,* [27] *but only a fearful expectation of judgment and of raging fire that will consume the enemies of God. (NIV)*

So thorough is God's consuming fire of judgment that it will leave them with neither root nor branch. In a forest fire, for example, the root is generally protected by its subsurface location--but not in this case. The intensity of God's judgment will consume them totally, root and branch.

Those who have embraced evil will be burned as stubble, their lifetime's accomplishments proving to have little enduring value on the day of testing. The point is they are not to be envied, but pitied.

Later revelation clarified the time of this judgment, which will be at the end of the millennium. We read the specifics in Revelation 20:11-15.

> [11] *Then I saw a great white throne and Him who sat upon it, from whose presence earth and heaven fled away, and no place was found for them.* [12] *And I saw the*

dead, the great and the small, standing before the throne, and books were opened; and another book was opened, which is the book of life; and the dead were judged from the things which were written in the books, according to their deeds. ^{13} And the sea gave up the dead which were in it, and death and Hades gave up the dead which were in them; and they were judged, every one of them according to their deeds. ^{14} Then death and Hades were thrown into the lake of fire. This is the second death, the lake of fire. ^{15} And if anyone's name was not found written in the book of life, he was thrown into the lake of fire.

And 2 Peter 3:10-13.

^{10} *But the day of the Lord will come like a thief, in which the heavens will pass away with a roar and the elements will be destroyed with intense heat, and the earth and its works will be burned up. ^{11} Since all these things are to be destroyed in this way, what sort of people ought you to be in holy conduct and godliness, ^{12} looking for and hastening the coming of the day of God, because of which the heavens will be destroyed by burning, and the elements will melt with intense heat! ^{13} But according to His promise we are looking for new heavens and a new earth, in which righteousness dwells.*

> We are not to envy the wicked because of their seemingly blessed condition in the present. We are to pity the wicked because of what they will experience in the future.

But there is yet a way of escape. If a person in this condition would repent of their sins and turn to Jesus Christ in faith, trusting only in His death and resurrection as their only hope of salvation, they will escape this fiery Day of Judgment. We see God speak this truth to us in John 5:24.

> *"Truly, truly, I say to you, he who hears My word, and believes Him who sent Me, has eternal life, and does not come into judgment, but has passed out of death into life.*

And Romans 8:1.

> *Therefore there is now no condemnation for those who are in Christ Jesus.*

We are not to envy the wicked because of their seemingly blessed condition in the present. We are to pity the wicked because of what they will experience in the future.

The Healing of God's Righteousness

Let's move to Malachi 4:2-3.

> *2 "But for you who fear My name, the sun of righteousness will rise with healing in its wings; and you will go forth and skip about like calves from the stall. 3 You will tread down the wicked, for they will be ashes under the soles of your feet on the day which I am preparing," says the Lord of hosts.*

"But" in contrast, on the day of the Lord, those who fear the Lord will experience the gentle healing wings, or rays of the sun

of righteousness and not the blasting heat of the furnace of
God's judgment.

Many Bible scholars believe that this is a reference to the
Messiah who is referred to in Scriptures as the Lord our
righteousness. But I see this as a reference to the condition of
righteousness which heals us from all the illnesses that sin has
brought into our lives and especially of sins condemnation.

It is a reference to that condition of standing right with God on
the basis of our faith in Christ alone. The condition of being
right with God, not on the basis of our merit, but on the merits
of Christ.

It is that righteousness that the Apostle Paul tells us--in
Philippians 3:8-9--that he wants to be found possessing on the
day of God's judgment.

> [8] *More than that, I count all things to be loss in view of
> the surpassing value of knowing Christ Jesus my Lord,
> for whom I have suffered the loss of all things, and count
> them but rubbish so that I may gain Christ,* [9] *and may be
> found in Him, not having a righteousness of my own
> derived from the Law, but that which is through faith in
> Christ, the righteousness which comes from God on the
> basis of faith.*

Romans 1:16-17 tells us it is the righteousness that is found in
the gospel.

> [16] *For I am not ashamed of the gospel, for it is the power
> of God for salvation to everyone who believes, to the
> Jew first and also to the Greek.* [17] *For in it the*

THE DANGER OF BEING DISAPPOINTED WITH GOD

righteousness of God is revealed from faith to faith; as it is written, "But the righteous man shall live by faith."

It is the righteousness of God that is the only righteousness that He will accept in order for sinful people to be made right with Him. It is not self-righteousness, nor is it a righteousness that is earned meritoriously. It is the righteousness of God, and from God, which is imputed to us on the basis of faith alone.

And on that day, when we believers enter into the fullness of that righteousness in the eternal state, we will be like calves that have been penned up in the stall for some time but now have been released into the open field which is full of sunshine.

> **Imputation?**
>
> Imputation refers to charging or reckoning something that belongs to another, to a person's account. A great example of this would be Paul's wanting Philemon to put to Paul's account any debt owed to Philemon by the runaway slave, Onesimus.
>
> (See Philemon 18)

We will be joyously skipping about having been released from the stall of a sin-cursed world.

And those wicked people that some of us envied in this fallen world because of their seemingly carefree lives, and their abundance of material blessings, and their status, power and prestige, will be ashes under the soles of our feet that we tread upon as we skip about in the joy of the sun of righteousness.

This not only indicates the finality of the judgment on the wicked, but it also brings to a sharp conclusion the answer in this oracle to the cynical question asked by the unfaithful Israelites, "What do we gain by carrying out His requirements?"

Consider the contrasting destinies. This is the antidote to being envious of those who do not know the Lord and yet seem prosperous and carefree in this life.

The Heeding of God's Law

Next, we look at Malachi 4:4.

> *Remember the law of Moses My servant, even the statutes and ordinances which I commanded him in Horeb for all Israel.*

To "remember" in the Old Testament means more than just simple recollection--it is the marriage of recollection and practical application. In the original language this is written as an imperative. It is a command to remember the Law of Moses by way of its application to their lives.

So it's more than just getting it into the mind, it's getting God's law into their lives practically.

The Jews of Malachi's day do not remember the Law as evidenced by their disobedience of the Law in terms of the sacrifices they present to the Lord. They show contempt for the Lord's sacrificial requirements by presenting lame and sickly animals to Him, something the Law strictly forbids.

They disregard the covenant of the Law by breaking faith with one another and by divorcing their wives in order to marry pagan women, something strictly forbidden in the Law of Moses.

They disobey God's Law in terms of the required giving of tithes and offerings.

And they disobey the Law of God in that they do not honor God with the kind of respect, awe, reverence and apprehension that He alone deserves.

But those who fear the Lord are to be careful to remember the Law of Moses, the decrees and Laws that God had given all of Israel on Mt. Sinai (Horeb).
Those of us who know Jesus as Lord and Savior are to remember the Law as well--not as the instrument of our salvation, but as our standards for living righteously in this present world.

R.C. Sproul, in his book Essential Truths of the Christian Faith, said of God's Law, "By studying or meditating on the law of God, we attend the school of righteousness. We learn what pleases God and what offends Him. The moral law that God reveals in Scripture is always binding upon us. Our redemption is from the curse of God's law, not from our duty to obey it. We are justified, not because of our obedience to the law, but in order that we may become obedient to God's law. To love Christ is to keep His commandments. To love God is to obey His law."

The Healer of Broken Relationships

Let's move to Malachi 4:5-6, the final two verses of the book of Malachi.

> [5] *Behold, I am going to send you Elijah the prophet before the coming of the great and terrible day of the Lord.* [6] *He will restore the hearts of the fathers to their*

*children and the hearts of the children to their fathers,
so that I will not come and smite the land with a curse.*

This promise of the coming of the prophet Elijah before the coming of the great and terrible day of the Lord presents a difficult interpretive challenge. This is the only passage in the whole of the Old Testament that speaks of this future ministry of this ancient prophet.

Many commentators link this prophecy with the messenger mentioned in Malachi 3:1. We have noted in a previous chapter that Matthew 11:7-10 clearly and specifically states that John the Baptist is the messenger spoken of in Malachi 3:1. It was John who prepared the way for the first coming of our Lord.

Elijah the prophet mentioned in Malachi 4:5-6 is the forerunner to the Second Coming of Christ and the great and terrible day of the Lord when our Lord pours out his wrath upon sinful humanity at his Second-Coming.

The solution is found in Matthew 17 where we have the record of the transfiguration of our Lord with Peter, James and John as the witnesses of this incredible event. It's important to keep in mind that these words were spoken after John the Baptist had been beheaded.

[1] Six days later Jesus took with Him Peter and James and John his brother, and led them up on a high mountain by themselves. [2] And He was transfigured before them; and His face shone like the sun, and His garments became as white as light. [3] And behold, Moses and Elijah appeared to them, talking with Him. [4] Peter said to Jesus, "Lord, it is good for us to be here; if You wish, I will make three tabernacles here, one for You,

and one for Moses, and one for Elijah." [5] *While he was still speaking, a bright cloud overshadowed them, and behold, a voice out of the cloud said, "This is My beloved Son, with whom I am well-pleased; listen to Him!"* [6] *When the disciples heard this, they fell face down to the ground and were terrified.* [7] *And Jesus came to them and touched them and said, "Get up, and do not be afraid."* [8] *And lifting up their eyes, they saw no one except Jesus Himself alone.* [9] *As they were coming down from the mountain, Jesus commanded them, saying, "Tell the vision to no one until the Son of Man has risen from the dead."* [10] *And His disciples asked Him, "Why then do the scribes say that Elijah must come first?"* [11] *And He answered and said, "Elijah is coming and will restore all things;* [12] *but I say to you that Elijah already came, and they did not recognize him, but did to him whatever they wished. So also the Son of Man is going to suffer at their hands."* [13] *Then the disciples understood that He had spoken to them about John the Baptist.*

John the Baptist came in the spirit and power of Elijah. But Elijah will come prior to the Second Coming of the Lord and His fierce judgment of this world at the end of the Tribulation.

The most likely New Testament reference to this future Elijah-like ministry is Revelation 11:1-13, which speaks of the two witnesses in the Tribulation.

[1] *Then there was given me a measuring rod like a staff; and someone said, "Get up and measure the temple of God and the altar, and those who worship in it.* [2] *"Leave out the court which is outside the temple and do not measure it, for it has been given to the nations; and they*

*will tread under foot the holy city for forty-two months. [3]
"And I will grant authority to my two witnesses, and they
will prophesy for twelve hundred and sixty days, clothed
in sackcloth." [4] These are the two olive trees and the two
lampstands that stand before the Lord of the earth. [5] And
if anyone wants to harm them, fire flows out of their
mouth and devours their enemies; so if anyone wants to
harm them, he must be killed in this way. [6] These have
the power to shut up the sky, so that rain will not fall
during the days of their prophesying; and they have
power over the waters to turn them into blood, and to
strike the earth with every plague, as often as they
desire. [7] When they have finished their testimony, the
beast that comes up out of the abyss will make war with
them, and overcome them and kill them. [8] And their dead
bodies will lie in the street of the great city which
mystically is called Sodom and Egypt, where also their
Lord was crucified. [9] Those from the peoples and tribes
and tongues and nations will look at their dead bodies
for three and a half days, and will not permit their dead
bodies to be laid in a tomb. [10] And those who dwell on
the earth will rejoice over them and celebrate; and they
will send gifts to one another, because these two
prophets tormented those who dwell on the earth. [11] But
after the three and a half days, the breath of life from
God came into them, and they stood on their feet; and
great fear fell upon those who were watching them. [12]
And they heard a loud voice from heaven saying to them,
"Come up here." Then they went up into heaven in the
cloud, and their enemies watched them. [13] And in that
hour there was a great earthquake, and a tenth of the
city fell; seven thousand people were killed in the
earthquake, and the rest were terrified and gave glory to
the God of heaven.*

THE DANGER OF BEING DISAPPOINTED WITH GOD

In any event, Elijah's arrival will be the precursor to the great and terrible day of the Lord--which in this context refers to the future time of ultimate judgment which is described in the New Testament as a day of wrath, and the great day of Almighty God when full and complete justice will be revealed in the exercise of His perfect judgment.

The Day of the Lord is expressed in the end times at the end of the Tribulation and at the end of the Millennium.

Yet, Malachi 4:5 leads to verse 6.

When our relationship with God is not right, other valued relationships in life tend to get out of order as well or feel the impact of our separation from God. The ministry of the coming prophet Elijah will be to bring about the kind of reconciliation with the Lord that provides restoration of family relationships.

Repentance and turning to God will be seen in the turning of the hearts of the fathers to their children and the hearts of the children to their fathers.

By the way, this principle is certainly true today. Nothing brings families closer than when they have a relationship with our Lord in common.

This ministry of restoration by the coming prophet Elijah will preserve the land (The Promised Land), from being devoted to total destruction under the curse of God.

Malachi closes this little book with an emphasis upon the heat of God's coming judgment experienced by those who are arrogant and evildoers, the healing of God's righteousness experienced by those who fear the Lord, a command to heed the

THE ORACLE OF MALACHI

law of the Lord and a prophetic declaration about the prophet
Elijah who will come as a healer of valued relationships just
before the great and terrible day of the Lord.

The Lord graciously has given mankind plenty of warnings
about the coming dreadful Day of the Lord when the wrath of
God is unleashed in the exercise of His righteous judgment. The
only way to escape the terror of that Day is by turning to Christ
to liberate you from the condemnation to come.

We are promised this in John 3:36.

> *He who believes in the Son has eternal life; but he who
> does not obey the Son will not see life, but the wrath of
> God abides on him.*

And in John 5:24.

> *Truly, truly, I say to you, he who hears My word, and
> believes Him who sent Me, has eternal life, and does not
> come into judgment, but has passed out of death into
> life.*

And the best way to be delivered from the spiritual corruption
of envying the wicked is to remember their destiny in contrast
with that of those who know the Lord. Take some time to read
Psalm 73 and Romans 8:18 when these thoughts cross your
mind. Proverbs 23:17 also gives us great guidance here.

> *Do not let your heart envy sinners, But live in the fear of
> the Lord always.*

And always remember the end.

THE DANGER OF BEING DISAPPOINTED WITH GOD

The last verse of Malachi, chapter 4 verse 6, shows us that familial reconciliation is greatly enhanced when people are reconciled with the Lord and share in the common bonding of being in Christ.

THE ORACLE OF MALACHI

Chapter 10
The Oracle Points

There is a direct correlation between your attitude toward God and your level of dedication and the quality of your service directed toward Him. What you think about God is the most important thing you think. Nothing will corrupt your mindset toward Him any quicker than being disappointed with your lot in life, angry about a certain circumstance or if you adopt the perception that the lost people of this world have it better than you do. Read Psalm 73 for a very clear example of this mental struggle and what our attitudes should be.

The truthfulness of the above statement is illustrated for us by the Jews of Malachi's day. Let's review what the Jews are experiencing at this time. They have been back in the Promised Land for about one hundred years. Because of the prophecies of Isaiah, Jeremiah and Ezekiel, they had anticipated a full restoration of the glory days experienced by those who lived under King David and King Solomon. They had imagined that they would be enjoying the Millennium blessings by now. However, they remain under Persian rule.

The temple has been rebuilt, but it lacks the beauty and splendor of Solomon's temple which had been destroyed during the captivity. Instead of being victorious in war and overflowing with the abundance of God's blessings, they are experiencing poverty, drought and economic adversity. Because God's timing is not their timing, and because God's plan conflicts with their wishes, they have become disappointed with Jehovah God.

THE ORACLE OF MALACHI

This mind-set causes them to be careless in their worship, indifferent to the truth, stingy in their offerings and unfaithful in upholding the Law of God.

And this all began with an attitude.

Always keep in mind that our attitudes in life always give way to our actions of life. Your daily attitude is one of the few things that you can choose. You can't choose the weather, or choose not to experience the uncertainties of any given day. But you can choose your attitude and your responses to the events in your life.

The example of the Jews of Malachi's day serves as a reminder to all genuine believers that you must not view God--or formulate your attitude toward Him--through the grid of unfavorable life circumstances, unreliable feelings or subjective perceptions of life. God, and indeed all of life, must be viewed through the perfect grid of the Scriptures.

This means I must know the perfections of God as He has disclosed them to me in His Word. I must understand what it means to my life that God is holy, sovereign, just, merciful, gracious, all knowing, all seeing, all powerful, all wise, self sufficient and eternal. I must know how to practically apply these truths and understand how these wonderful attributes of God should serve as my reliable navigator as I maneuver my way through the unpredictability of life's circumstances and all the disappoints we encounter under the sun.

The truth that God works all things for the good to those who love Him and are called according to His purpose, as revealed in Romans 8:28, must be more than a verse I can quote. It must be a firm foundation upon which I can take my stand as I encounter the tumultuous sea of life in a fallen world.

The Jews of Malachi's day also illustrate that there is a correlation between your attitude toward God and His Word and how you treat the precious relationships that you have in this life; in particular, your marriage relationship.

When our vertical relationship is out of order, our horizontal relationships tend to suffer the backwash of that situation. This is illustrated by the men of Israel who deceptively maneuver their way out of their previously ratified marriage covenant with the wife of their youth in order to marry pagan women, as we read in Malachi 2:11-16, and discussed in chapter 5 of this book. And yet they maintain the practice of offering sacrifices to God which He rejects and they are perplexed by God's disfavor with their offerings.

This should remind us of the truth that your relationship with your mate in marriage is directly impacted by the condition of your relationship with the Creator of marriage. We must always take note of the fact that God is far more interested in you conducting your marriage in accordance with His will, than your external expressions of religious devotion.

God is the creator of marriage and He hates divorce because He hates the source of divorce--which is sin expressed in self-centeredness and pride. For those of us who are married, it's important to keep in mind that the mandates for how we are to conduct ourselves in marriage must be obeyed because they are the will of God for us in this context.

We can see these mandates in Ephesians 5:22-33.

²² Wives, be subject to your own husbands, as to the Lord. ²³ For the husband is the head of the wife, as Christ also is the head of the church, He Himself being the Savior of the body. ²⁴ But as the church is subject to Christ, so also the wives ought to be to their husbands in everything. ²⁵ Husbands, love your wives, just as Christ also loved the church and gave Himself up for her, ²⁶ so that He might sanctify her, having cleansed her by the washing of water with the word, ²⁷ that He might present to Himself the church in all her glory, having no spot or wrinkle or any such thing; but that she would be holy and blameless. ²⁸ So husbands ought also to love their own wives as their own bodies. He who loves his own wife loves himself; ²⁹ for no one ever hated his own flesh, but nourishes and cherishes it, just as Christ also does the church, ³⁰ because we are members of His body. ³¹ For this reason a man shall leave his father and mother and shall be joined to his wife, and the two shall become one flesh. ³² This mystery is great; but I am speaking with reference to Christ and the church. ³³ Nevertheless, each individual among you also is to love his own wife even as himself, and the wife must see to it that she respects her husband.

> **Your relationship with your mate in marriage is directly impacted by the condition of your relationship with the Creator of marriage.**

And Colossians 3:18-19.

¹⁸ Wives, be subject to your husbands, as is fitting in the Lord. ¹⁹ Husbands, love your wives and do not be embittered against them.

If you condition your obedience on your mate's submission or lack of submission to the mandates of marriage, you will disobey the

THE DANGER OF BEING DISAPPOINTED WITH GOD

Lord. You obey the Lord because you love the Lord, as seen in John 14:15.

> *If you love Me, you will keep My commandments.*

And 1 John 5:2-3.

> *[2] By this we know that we love the children of God, when we love God and observe His commandments. [3] For this is the love of God, that we keep His commandments; and His commandments are not burdensome.*

You must not disobey the Lord because of your mate's disobedience.

Hebrews 13:4 gives us more guidance.

> *Marriage is to be held in honor among all, and the marriage bed is to be undefiled; for fornicators and adulterers God will judge.*

As a husband who desires to honor the Lord with my marriage, I must grow in the grace and the knowledge of the Lord. I must be focused on maintaining the priority of spiritual disciplines, such as the study of the Word, meditation on the Word and the willful application of the Word, in order to deepen my intimacy with Christ. I must give myself to the continuous advancement toward Christlikeness. My marriage, my family and my church depend upon me growing up in all things in the Lord.

Another very important lesson that emerges from the book of Malachi is that the level of your dedication to the Lord and the quality of your service done in His name is a pretty good indicator of the condition of your relationship with Him. The condition of the relationship between the priests of Israel and the Lord was at an all time low during the days of Malachi. The evidence of this is manifested in their willingness to offer to God flea-bitten, blind and half dead animals that they would never think of offering to their governor, as we read in Malachi 1:6-8.

In addition, the people are robbing God of the mandated tithes and offerings and have placed themselves under God's curse because of this action as we saw in Malachi 3:8-12. This not only indicates their lack of love for the Lord and His will, but also their inability to trust the Lord to make the kind of provisions to them that enables them to be generous and willing to share on every occasion.

I need to ask myself, what does my current level of dedication and service done in the name of Lord indicate about the current condition of my relationship with Him? If I profess to love the Lord, does my conduct confirm my claim? If I say I trust the Lord to provide what I need and to enable me to share with others, would my giving support my profession? If I declare that my great desire is to serve the Lord for His glory and honor, is that the true motivation of my heart?

In the book of Revelation, the Lord addresses the church in Ephesus about the issue of leaving their first love. The Love for God and others that served as the catalysis for all that they did in ministry. The Lord declares to them, in Revelation 2:4, that their love for Him and others has greatly diminished.

But I have this against you, that you have left your first love.

THE DANGER OF BEING DISAPPOINTED WITH GOD

This comes as a shock to this church because Revelation 2:1-3 tells us they are so orthodox, discerning and persevering in the face of persecution.

> *¹ To the angel of the church in Ephesus write: The One who holds the seven stars in His right hand, the One who walks among the seven golden lampstands, says this: ² "I know your deeds and your toil and perseverance, and that you cannot tolerate evil men, and you put to the test those who call themselves apostles, and they are not, and you found them to be false; ³ and you have perseverance and have endured for My name's sake, and have not grown weary."*

Yet in reality, their relationship with the Lord is not in good shape.

Jesus provides them a strategy for getting that initial first love vitality back into their hearts. It requires that they have to come to grips with the reality of their current spiritual condition. Revelation 3:5 tells us they are to remember from where they have fallen.

God is perfect. His ways are perfect. His timing is perfect. The outworking of His providence is a manifestation of His perfect wisdom working in partnership with His sovereignty.

He who overcomes will thus be clothed in white garments; and I will not erase his name from the book of life, and I will confess his name before My Father and before His angels.

This requires acknowledging that things aren't what they used to be. A change and renewal has to take place.

Secondly, they need to repent. They need to undergo a radical change of mind about those attitudes and mind-sets that have corrupted their love relationship with the Lord.

And finally, they are to do those things that they did at first, when their first love was at its zenith.

No doubt this involves such things as knowing and obeying the Word of God, joyfully serving others in the name of Christ and actively sharing the Gospel with others. It is interesting to me that the Lord doesn't tell this church to try to cultivate a feeling of intimacy with Him. He instructs them to repeat the things that created the sense of first love intimacy with Him. Jesus says that those who are more intimate with Him than His mother or brothers are those who listen intently to His word and obey it, as recorded in Luke 8:19-21.

> [19] *And His mother and brothers came to Him, and they were unable to get to Him because of the crowd.* [20] *And it was reported to Him, "Your mother and Your brothers are standing outside, wishing to see You."* [21] *But He answered and said to them, "My mother and My brothers are these who hear the word of God and do it."*

And Luke 11:27-28.

> [27] *While Jesus was saying these things, one of the women in the crowd raised her voice and said to Him, "Blessed is the womb that bore You and the breasts at which You nursed."* [28] *But He said, "On the contrary, blessed are those who hear the word of God and observe it."*

God is perfect. His ways are perfect. His timing is perfect. The outworking of His providence is a manifestation of His perfect wisdom working in partnership with His sovereignty. I certainly don't know all about why God does what He does and why He has selected a certain time to do what He does. King Solomon, the wisest man who ever lived says in Ecclesiastes 8:16-17 that if someone declares that they have discovered why God does what He does under the sun, he really does not know.

> *[16] When I applied my mind to know wisdom and to observe man's labor on earth, his eyes not seeing sleep day or night, [17] then I saw all that God has done. No one can comprehend what goes on under the sun. Despite all his efforts to search it out, man cannot discover its meaning. Even if a wise man claims he knows, he cannot really comprehend it. (NIV)*

But I am certain of the fact that what He does and when He does it is altogether righteous and should prompt us to glorify Him.

There is indeed a real danger to being disappointed with God, His timing and His purposes. It can severely corrupt your relationship with the Lord and cause you to step beyond His will. Cain was disappointed with God regarding his sacrifice and murdered his brother Abel as recorded in Genesis 4:1-8.

> *[1] Now the man had relations with his wife Eve, and she conceived and gave birth to Cain, and she said, "I have gotten a manchild with the help of the Lord." [2] Again, she gave birth to his brother Abel. And Abel was a keeper of flocks, but Cain was a tiller of the ground. [3] So it came about in the course of time that Cain brought an offering to the Lord of the fruit of the ground. [4] Abel, on his part also brought of the firstlings of his flock and of their fat portions And the Lord had regard for Abel and*

for his offering; ⁵ but for Cain and for his offering He had no regard. So Cain became very angry and his countenance fell. ⁶ Then the Lord said to Cain, "Why are you angry? And why has your countenance fallen? ⁷ If you do well, will not your countenance be lifted up? And if you do not do well, sin is crouching at the door; and its desire is for you, but you must master it." ⁸ Cain told Abel his brother. And it came about when they were in the field, that Cain rose up against Abel his brother and killed him.

Abraham and Sarah apparently grew impatient with waiting for God to fulfill His promise of a son. And Genesis 16:1-15 records how they came up with a culturally practiced plan that has negatively impacted the nation of Israel to this very day.

¹ Now Sarai, Abram's wife had borne him no children, and she had an Egyptian maid whose name was Hagar. ² So Sarai said to Abram, "Now behold, the Lord has prevented me from bearing children. Please go in to my maid; perhaps I will obtain children through her." And Abram listened to the voice of Sarai. ³ After Abram had lived ten years in the land of Canaan, Abram's wife Sarai took Hagar the Egyptian, her maid, and gave her to her husband Abram as his wife. ⁴ He went in to Hagar, and she conceived; and when she saw that she had conceived, her mistress was despised in her sight. ⁵ And Sarai said to Abram, "May the wrong done me be upon you. I gave my maid into your arms, but when she saw that she had conceived, I was despised in her sight. May the Lord judge between you and me." ⁶ But Abram said to Sarai, "Behold, your maid is in your power; do to her what is good in your sight." So Sarai treated her harshly, and she fled from her presence. ⁷ Now the angel

THE DANGER OF BEING DISAPPOINTED WITH GOD

*of the Lord found her by a spring of water in the
wilderness, by the spring on the way to Shur. [8] He said,
"Hagar, Sarai's maid, where have you come from and
where are you going?" And she said, "I am fleeing from
the presence of my mistress Sarai." [9] Then the angel of
the Lord said to her, "Return to your mistress, and
submit yourself to her authority." [10] Moreover, the angel
of the Lord said to her, "I will greatly multiply your
descendants so that they will be too many to count." [11]
The angel of the Lord said to her further, "Behold, you
are with child, And you will bear a son; And you shall
call his name Ishmael, Because the Lord has given heed
to your affliction. [12] He will be a wild donkey of a
man, His hand will be against everyone, And everyone's
hand will be against him; And he will live to the east of
all his brothers." [13] Then she called the name of the Lord
who spoke to her, "You are a God who sees"; for she
said, "Have I even remained alive here after seeing
Him?" [14] Therefore the well was called Beer-lahai-roi;
behold, it is between Kadesh and Bered. [15] So Hagar
bore Abram a son; and Abram called the name of his
son, whom Hagar bore, Ishmael.*

How about you?

Have you learned to be content with your circumstances in life
because of your trust in God's sovereignty and love?

What does your service that you do in the name of the Lord say
about your mind-set toward the Lord and His will?

How about your marriage?

How about your giving?

THE ORACLE OF MALACHI

Do you love the Lord supremely, trust the Lord unreservedly and stand upon His Word without compromise or equivocation?

I trust that your life and the activities of your life communicate the message that your faith rests in the person, work and Word of the Lord--and not in your circumstances or your feelings.

I must bring this book to a close by asking you if you know the Lord Jesus Christ as your Savior. Has there been a point in your life when you came to grips with the reality that you are a sinner, separated from a Holy God because of your sin and without the resources to fix the problem of sin?

In most cases throughout this book I have given you the Scriptures I have referenced, as it is essential you don't take my word for it. You must base your decision on what God says in His Word, and to do that you must read it. Now, I ask you to grab a Bible and look up Romans 3:23, Ecclesiastes 7:20 and 1 John 1:8-10. Seriously! Stop, and grab a Bible!

No amount of good works, religious rituals such as baptism, christening or keeping sacraments will satisfy your sin debt to God. That is why He graciously and mercifully sent His Son into this world to be the Savior of the world.

Read 1 John 4:14, 1 Timothy 1:15 and Luke 19:10. Now that you've read them, we can continue.

The glorious good news is that Jesus died for our sins, sufficiently paying our debt of sin and liberating all who trust in His saving work from the condemnation and curse of sin.

Read Romans 8:1.

THE DANGER OF BEING DISAPPOINTED WITH GOD

Jesus rose from the dead, conquering death for all who totally trust in what He has done for us. You can read this truth in 1 Corinthians 15:1-5. Please look it up, and then we can continue.

Romans 10:9–10 tells you what to do now.

> [9] *that if you confess with your mouth Jesus as Lord, and believe in your heart that God raised Him from the dead, you will be saved;* [10] *for with the heart a person believes, resulting in righteousness, and with the mouth he confesses, resulting in salvation.*

This is what matters. You can get some great life truths from this book, but none of it really matters if you eternal destination is not secured. Trusting in Jesus Christ as your Lord and Savior is the first step you need to take towards thinking correctly about the person and purposes of God.

And the transformation of your life can then start to take place.

Welcome to the journey of a lifetime.

THE ORACLE OF MALACHI

The Book of Malachi
New American Standard Bible (NASB)

Malachi 1

God's Love for Jacob

[1] The oracle of the word of the Lord to Israel through Malachi.

[2] "I have loved you," says the Lord. But you say, "How have You loved us?" "Was not Esau Jacob's brother?" declares the Lord, "Yet I have loved Jacob;

[3] but I have hated Esau, and I have made his mountains a desolation and appointed his inheritance for the jackals of the wilderness."

[4] Though Edom says, "We have been beaten down, but we will return and build up the ruins"; thus says the Lord of hosts, "They may build, but I will tear down; and men will call them the wicked territory, and the people toward whom the Lord is indignant forever."

[5] Your eyes will see this and you will say, "The Lord be magnified beyond the border of Israel!"

Sin of the Priests

[6] " 'A son honors his father, and a servant his master. Then if I am a father, where is My honor? And if I am a master, where is My respect?' says the Lord of hosts to you, O priests who

despise My name. But you say, 'How have we despised Your name?'

⁷ "You are presenting defiled food upon My altar. But you say, 'How have we defiled You?' In that you say, 'The table of the Lord is to be despised.'

⁸ "But when you present the blind for sacrifice, is it not evil? And when you present the lame and sick, is it not evil? Why not offer it to your governor? Would he be pleased with you? Or would he receive you kindly?" says the Lord of hosts.

⁹ "But now will you not entreat God's favor, that He may be gracious to us? With such an offering on your part, will He receive any of you kindly?" says the Lord of hosts.

¹⁰ "Oh that there were one among you who would shut the gates, that you might not uselessly kindle fire on My altar! I am not pleased with you," says the Lord of hosts, "nor will I accept an offering from you.

¹¹ "For from the rising of the sun even to its setting, My name will be great among the nations, and in every place incense is going to be offered to My name, and a grain offering that is pure; for My name will be great among the nations," says the Lord of hosts.

¹² "But you are profaning it, in that you say, 'The table of the Lord is defiled, and as for its fruit, its food is to be despised.'

¹³ "You also say, 'My, how tiresome it is!' And you disdainfully sniff at it," says the Lord of hosts, "and you bring what was taken by robbery and what is lame or sick; so you bring the offering! Should I receive that from your hand?" says the Lord.

[14] "But cursed be the swindler who has a male in his flock and vows it, but sacrifices a blemished animal to the Lord, for I am a great King," says the Lord of hosts, "and My name is feared among the nations."

Malachi 2

Priests to Be Disciplined

[1] "And now this commandment is for you, O priests.

[2] "If you do not listen, and if you do not take it to heart to give honor to My name," says the Lord of hosts, "then I will send the curse upon you and I will curse your blessings; and indeed, I have cursed them already, because you are not taking it to heart.

[3] "Behold, I am going to rebuke your offspring, and I will spread refuse on your faces, the refuse of your feasts; and you will be taken away with it.

[4] "Then you will know that I have sent this commandment to you, that My covenant may continue with Levi," says the Lord of hosts.

[5] "My covenant with him was one of life and peace, and I gave them to him as an object of reverence; so he revered Me and stood in awe of My name.

[6] "True instruction was in his mouth and unrighteousness was not found on his lips; he walked with Me in peace and uprightness, and he turned many back from iniquity.

THE ORACLE OF MALACHI

⁷ "For the lips of a priest should preserve knowledge, and men should seek instruction from his mouth; for he is the messenger of the Lord of hosts.

⁸ "But as for you, you have turned aside from the way; you have caused many to stumble by the instruction; you have corrupted the covenant of Levi," says the Lord of hosts.

⁹ "So I also have made you despised and abased before all the people, just as you are not keeping My ways but are showing partiality in the instruction.

Sin in the Family

¹⁰ "Do we not all have one father? Has not one God created us? Why do we deal treacherously each against his brother so as to profane the covenant of our fathers?

¹¹ "Judah has dealt treacherously, and an abomination has been committed in Israel and in Jerusalem; for Judah has profaned the sanctuary of the Lord which He loves and has married the daughter of a foreign god.

¹² "As for the man who does this, may the Lord cut off from the tents of Jacob everyone who awakes and answers, or who presents an offering to the Lord of hosts.

¹³ "This is another thing you do: you cover the altar of the Lord with tears, with weeping and with groaning, because He no longer regards the offering or accepts it with favor from your hand.

¹⁴ "Yet you say, 'For what reason?' Because the Lord has been a witness between you and the wife of your youth, against whom

you have dealt treacherously, though she is your companion and your wife by covenant.

¹⁵ "But not one has done so who has a remnant of the Spirit. And what did that one do while he was seeking a godly offspring? Take heed then to your spirit, and let no one deal treacherously against the wife of your youth.

¹⁶ "For I hate divorce," says the Lord, the God of Israel, "and him who covers his garment with wrong," says the Lord of hosts. "So take heed to your spirit, that you do not deal treacherously."

¹⁷ You have wearied the Lord with your words. Yet you say, "How have we wearied Him?" In that you say, "Everyone who does evil is good in the sight of the Lord, and He delights in them," or, "Where is the God of justice?"

Malachi 3

The Purifier

¹ "Behold, I am going to send My messenger, and he will clear the way before Me And the Lord, whom you seek, will suddenly come to His temple; and the messenger of the covenant, in whom you delight, behold, He is coming," says the Lord of hosts.

² "But who can endure the day of His coming? And who can stand when He appears? For He is like a refiner's fire and like fullers' soap.

THE ORACLE OF MALACHI

³ "He will sit as a smelter and purifier of silver, and He will purify the sons of Levi and refine them like gold and silver, so that they may present to the Lord offerings in righteousness.

⁴ "Then the offering of Judah and Jerusalem will be pleasing to the Lord as in the days of old and as in former years.

⁵ "Then I will draw near to you for judgment; and I will be a swift witness against the sorcerers and against the adulterers and against those who swear falsely, and against those who oppress the wage earner in his wages, the widow and the orphan, and those who turn aside the alien and do not fear Me," says the Lord of hosts.

⁶ "For I, the Lord, do not change; therefore you, O sons of Jacob, are not consumed.

⁷ "From the days of your fathers you have turned aside from My statutes and have not kept them. Return to Me, and I will return to you," says the Lord of hosts. "But you say, 'How shall we return?'

You Have Robbed God

⁸ "Will a man rob God? Yet you are robbing Me! But you say, 'How have we robbed You?' In tithes and offerings.

⁹ "You are cursed with a curse, for you are robbing Me, the whole nation of you!

¹⁰ "Bring the whole tithe into the storehouse, so that there may be food in My house, and test Me now in this," says the Lord of hosts, "if I will not open for you the windows of heaven and pour out for you a blessing until it overflows.

[11] "Then I will rebuke the devourer for you, so that it will not destroy the fruits of the ground; nor will your vine in the field cast its grapes," says the Lord of hosts.

[12] "All the nations will call you blessed, for you shall be a delightful land," says the Lord of hosts.

[13] "Your words have been arrogant against Me," says the Lord. "Yet you say, 'What have we spoken against You?'

[14] "You have said, 'It is vain to serve God; and what profit is it that we have kept His charge, and that we have walked in mourning before the Lord of hosts?

[15] 'So now we call the arrogant blessed; not only are the doers of wickedness built up but they also test God and escape.'"

The Book of Remembrance

[16] Then those who feared the Lord spoke to one another, and the Lord gave attention and heard it, and a book of remembrance was written before Him for those who fear the Lord and who esteem His name.

[17] "They will be Mine," says the Lord of hosts, "on the day that I prepare My own possession, and I will spare them as a man spares his own son who serves him."

[18] So you will again distinguish between the righteous and the wicked, between one who serves God and one who does not serve Him.

THE ORACLE OF MALACHI

Malachi 4

Final Admonition

[1] "For behold, the day is coming, burning like a furnace; and all the arrogant and every evildoer will be chaff; and the day that is coming will set them ablaze," says the Lord of hosts, "so that it will leave them neither root nor branch."

[2] "But for you who fear My name, the sun of righteousness will rise with healing in its wings; and you will go forth and skip about like calves from the stall.

[3] "You will tread down the wicked, for they will be ashes under the soles of your feet on the day which I am preparing," says the Lord of hosts.

[4] "Remember the law of Moses My servant, even the statutes and ordinances which I commanded him in Horeb for all Israel.

[5] "Behold, I am going to send you Elijah the prophet before the coming of the great and terrible day of the Lord.

[6] "He will restore the hearts of the fathers to their children and the hearts of the children to their fathers, so that I will not come and smite the land with a curse."

The Book of Malachi
English Standard Version (ESV)

Malachi 1

¹The oracle of the word of the LORD to Israel by Malachi.

The LORD's Love for Israel

² "I have loved you," says the LORD. But you say, "How have you loved us?" "Is not Esau Jacob's brother?" declares the LORD. "Yet I have loved Jacob ³but Esau I have hated. I have laid waste his hill country and left his heritage to jackals of the desert." ⁴If Edom says, "We are shattered but we will rebuild the ruins," the LORD of hosts says, "They may build, but I will tear down, and they will be called 'the wicked country,' and 'the people with whom the LORD is angry forever.'" ⁵ Your own eyes shall see this, and you shall say, "Great is the LORD beyond the border of Israel!"

The Priests' Polluted Offerings

⁶ "A son honors his father, and a servant his master. If then I am a father, where is my honor? And if I am a master, where is my fear? says the LORD of hosts to you, O priests, who despise my name. But you say, 'How have we despised your name?' ⁷ By offering polluted food upon my altar. But you say, 'How have we polluted you?' By saying that the LORD's table may be despised. ⁸ When you offer blind animals in sacrifice, is that not evil? And when you offer those that are lame or sick, is that not evil? Present that to your governor; will he accept you or show you favor? says the LORD of hosts. ⁹And now entreat the favor of God, that he may be gracious to us. With such a gift from your hand, will he show favor to any of you? says the LORD of

hosts. [10] Oh that there were one among you who would shut the doors, that you might not kindle fire on my altar in vain! I have no pleasure in you, says the LORD of hosts, and I will not accept an offering from your hand. [11]For from the rising of the sun to its setting my name will be great among the nations, and in every place incense will be offered to my name, and a pure offering. For my name will be great among the nations, says the LORD of hosts. [12]But you profane it when you say that the Lord's table is polluted, and its fruit, that is, its food may be despised. [13]But you say, 'What a weariness this is,' and you snort at it, says the LORD of hosts. You bring what has been taken by violence or is lame or sick, and this you bring as your offering! Shall I accept that from your hand? says the LORD. [14]Cursed be the cheat who has a male in his flock, and vows it, and yet sacrifices to the Lord what is blemished. For I am a great King, says the LORD of hosts, and my name will be feared among the nations.

Malachi 2

The LORD Rebukes the Priests

[1]"And now, O priests, this command is for you. [2] If you will not listen, if you will not take it to heart to give honor to my name, says the LORD of hosts, then I will send the curse upon you and I will curse your blessings. Indeed, I have already cursed them, because you do not lay it to heart. [3]Behold, I will rebuke your offspring, and spread dung on your faces, the dung of your offerings, and you shall be taken away with it. [4]So shall you know that I have sent this command to you, that my covenant with Levi may stand, says the LORD of hosts. [5]My covenant with him was one of life and peace, and I gave them to him. It was a covenant of fear, and he feared me. He stood in awe of my name. [6] True instruction was in his mouth, and no

wrong was found on his lips. He walked with me in peace and uprightness, and he turned many from iniquity. [7]For the lips of a priest should guard knowledge, and people should seek instruction from his mouth, for he is the messenger of the LORD of hosts. [8]But you have turned aside from the way. You have caused many to stumble by your instruction. You have corrupted the covenant of Levi, says the LORD of hosts, [9]and so I make you despised and abased before all the people, inasmuch as you do not keep my ways but show partiality in your instruction."

Judah Profaned the Covenant

[10]Have we not all one Father? Has not one God created us? Why then are we faithless to one another, profaning the covenant of our fathers? [11]Judah has been faithless, and abomination has been committed in Israel and in Jerusalem. For Judah has profaned the sanctuary of the LORD, which he loves, and has married the daughter of a foreign god. [12]May the LORD cut off from the tents of Jacob any descendant of the man who does this, who brings an offering to the LORD of hosts!

[13]And this second thing you do. You cover the LORD's altar with tears, with weeping and groaning because he no longer regards the offering or accepts it with favor from your hand. [14] But you say, "Why does he not?" Because the LORD was witness between you and the wife of your youth, to whom you have been faithless, though she is your companion and your wife by covenant. [15] Did he not make them one, with a portion of the Spirit in their union? And what was the one God seeking? Godly offspring. So guard yourselves in your spirit, and let none of you be faithless to the wife of your youth. [16]"For the man who does not love his wife but divorces her, says the LORD, the God of Israel, covers his garment with violence,

says the LORD of hosts. So guard yourselves in your spirit, and do not be faithless."

The Messenger of the LORD

[17] You have wearied the LORD with your words. But you say, "How have we wearied him?" By saying, "Everyone who does evil is good in the sight of the LORD, and he delights in them." Or by asking, "Where is the God of justice?"

Malachi 3

[1] "Behold, I send my messenger, and he will prepare the way before me. And the Lord whom you seek will suddenly come to his temple; and the messenger of the covenant in whom you delight, behold, he is coming, says the LORD of hosts. [2]But who can endure the day of his coming, and who can stand when he appears? For he is like a refiner's fire and like fullers' soap. [3]He will sit as a refiner and purifier of silver, and he will purify the sons of Levi and refine them like gold and silver, and they will bring offerings in righteousness to the LORD. [4] Then the offering of Judah and Jerusalem will be pleasing to the LORD as in the days of old and as in former years.

[5]"Then I will draw near to you for judgment. I will be a swift witness against the sorcerers, against the adulterers, against those who swear falsely, against those who oppress the hired worker in his wages, the widow and the fatherless, against those who thrust aside the sojourner, and do not fear me, says the LORD of hosts.

THE DANGER OF BEING DISAPPOINTED WITH GOD

Robbing God

[6]"For I the LORD do not change; therefore you, O children of Jacob, are not consumed. [7] From the days of your fathers you have turned aside from my statutes and have not kept them. Return to me, and I will return to you, says the LORD of hosts. But you say, 'How shall we return?' [8]Will man rob God? Yet you are robbing me. But you say, 'How have we robbed you?' In your tithes and contributions. [9] You are cursed with a curse, for you are robbing me, the whole nation of you. [10] Bring the full tithe into the storehouse, that there may be food in my house. And thereby put me to the test, says the LORD of hosts, if I will not open the windows of heaven for you and pour down for you a blessing until there is no more need. [11]I will rebuke the devourer for you, so that it will not destroy the fruits of your soil, and your vine in the field shall not fail to bear, says the LORD of hosts. [12]Then all nations will call you blessed, for you will be a land of delight, says the LORD of hosts.

[13] "Your words have been hard against me, says the LORD. But you say, 'How have we spoken against you?' [14]You have said, 'It is vain to serve God. What is the profit of our keeping his charge or of walking as in mourning before the LORD of hosts? [15]And now we call the arrogant blessed. Evildoers not only prosper but they put God to the test and they escape.'"

The Book of Remembrance

[16]Then those who feared the LORD spoke with one another. The LORD paid attention and heard them, and a book of remembrance was written before him of those who feared the LORD and esteemed his name. [17]"They shall be mine, says the LORD of hosts, in the day when I make up my treasured possession, and I will spare them as a man spares his son who

serves him. [18]Then once more you shall see the distinction between the righteous and the wicked, between one who serves God and one who does not serve him.

Malachi 4

The Great Day of the LORD

[1] "For behold, the day is coming, burning like an oven, when all the arrogant and all evildoers will be stubble. The day that is coming shall set them ablaze, says the LORD of hosts, so that it will leave them neither root nor branch. [2]But for you who fear my name, the sun of righteousness shall rise with healing in its wings. You shall go out leaping like calves from the stall. [3]And you shall tread down the wicked, for they will be ashes under the soles of your feet, on the day when I act, says the LORD of hosts.

[4] "Remember the law of my servant Moses, the statutes and rules that I commanded him at Horeb for all Israel.

[5] "Behold, I will send you Elijah the prophet before the great and awesome day of the LORD comes. [6]And he will turn the hearts of fathers to their children and the hearts of children to their fathers, lest I come and strike the land with a decree of utter destruction."

About the Author

Pastor Jerry Marshall is a graduate of the Moody Bible Institute, Trinity College and has attended Trinity Seminary in Deerfield, Illinois. The original goal for his life was to become a professional musician.

Shortly after realizing his dream, he discovered that having "arrived" did not bring the joy or the fulfillment that he anticipated. Through a series of providentially-arranged circumstances, he came to a saving knowledge of Jesus Christ. Since that time, he has been passionate about knowing the Lord's Word and teaching it accurately.

Pastor Marshall's passion for assisting people to comprehend and apply God's Word through the vehicle of expository teaching is best articulated in Nehemiah 8:8,

> *"They read from the Book of the Law of God, making it clear and giving the meaning so that the people could understand what was being read."*

Pastor Marshall entered full time ministry in 1976. Through these years, Cindy, his wife since 1968, has faithfully served beside him as his life partner and gifted participant to the overall ministry. Together, they have three sons who are married and raising their own families.

Pastor Marshall is a gifted communicator who is dedicated to teaching God's Word one verse at a time. He has served at New Community Church in Wildwood, Missouri, since 1989.

Visit **www.MalachiBook.us** for additional resources and to contact Pastor Marshall.